Apocalypse

The Revelation
of
Jesus Christ

Dr. Ana Méndez Ferrell

Voice of The Light Ministries

THANKSGIVING & DEDICATION

I want to thank my heavenly Father, Jesus Christ and Holy Spirit for giving me the privilege to receive the revelations of this book. It is to my God in His three persons that I also dedicate this work.

PRAYER

I pray that the eyes of the understanding will be open in every person that reads this book and that they can glorify and know Jesus Christ the Messiah in the revelation of His Kingdom.

Voice Of The Light Ministries

Apocalypse, The Revelation of Jesus Christ

2012, 2016 Copyright © Ana Méndez Ferrell

All rights reserved. This publication may not be reproduced or transmitted in any form or any means, filed in an electronic system nor transmitted in any electronic, mechanical way including photocopying, recording or by any information storage retrieval system, or in any other manner (including audiobooks), without the previous written permission of the author.

Category	Reformation
Publisher	Voice of The Light Ministries
	P.O. Box 3418
	Ponte Vedra, Florida, 32004
	United States of America
	www.VoiceOfTheLight.com

ISBN 978-1-933163-83-3

2016 Revised & Expanded Edition

CONTENT

Foreword   9
Commentary   13

SECTION 1
THE BOOK OF REVELATION SEEN FROM THE PROPHETIC PERSPECTIVE OF THE KINGDOM OF GOD

1. My Experience In Patmos   19
2. The Dilemma of Interpretation   29
3. The Essence Of The Book of Revelation   39
4. The Power Of Preconceived Ideas   49
5. The Two Great Eras   55

SECTION 2
THE FUNDAMENTAL THEMES IN THE BOOK OF REVELATION

6. A New Heaven And A New Earth   71
7. The Work Of Messiah In His First Coming   83
8. God's Tabernacle with Man and The New Jerusalem   101
9. The Lamb's Spouse   121
10. Babylon, The Great Harlot   133
11. Victory Over Babylon   145
12. The Manifestation Of Jesus   163
13. The Abode Of God In The Clouds   173
14. Meeting The Lord In The Clouds   187
15. Heaven's Supreme Court   201
16. God's Judgments   217

Section 3
The Book Of Revelation's Secondary Subjects

17.	The Great Tribulation	237
18.	The Beast	243
19.	The Times In The Book Of Revelation	253
	Conclusion	259
	Blessing	259

Section 4
Appendixes/Instruments
(which will help you reach your own conclusions)

IN 1. Words describing Christ's Presence & His Second Coming	265
IN 2. The Times The Primitive Church Lived In	275
IN 3. The Signs of The End	281
IN 4. The Intermediate Coming of Christ by Apostle Fernando Orihuela	303
IN 5. The Order of The Book of Revelation	309

FOREWORD

BY
APOSTLE FERNANDO ORIHUELA

TIME FOR APOSTOLIC RE-CONSIDERATION:

"In Pursuit of A New Reformation"

A reform-pursuing Church needs to revisit "what they believe" and "why" they believe what they say "they believe."

Throughout the Church's history, there undoubtedly have been times where certain doctrinal points are considered "untouchable" and beyond any judgment or discussion. The first brethren were divided regarding the baptism of the Holy Spirit upon the Gentiles. The majority of them - and this thanks to the *Jerusalem* brethren- thought that the Greeks, Romans, and the rest of the converts from the *Mediterranean* and *Asia* could not be filled with this wonderful blessing. United to this thought was the fact that the concept about non-Jews who had professed their faith in Christ, had to be circumcised and even follow some of the Jewish regulations inherent to the Law, and the Old Covenant.

It was in the community of *Antioch* - the nucleus of the pioneer church- where the Jewish believers in Jesus had arrived; were shocked to see how the converted members had not been circumcised nor were they complying with other legal Jewish precepts. This is the reason the disciples in that city charged Paul and Barnabas along with "*certain other of them*" to go to *Jerusalem* to solve this situation once and for all.

It was at the *Jerusalem Council* where this matter was dealt with, along other faith points; this gave rise to the first regulatory meeting of the primitive church (towards the year 50 AD) according to the writings in Chapter 15 of the Book of Acts of the Apostles.

Their across-the-board resolution encompassed all groups of believers.

"For it seemed good to the Holy Ghost, and to us, to lay upon you no greater burden than these necessary things: that ye abstain from meats offered to idols, and from blood, and from things strangled, and from fornication. If ye keep yourselves from these things, ye shall do well. Fare ye well!"

Acts 15:28-29

Defining the issues in a conflict has not always been this easy. The controversy John Wesley had with the *Church of England* regarding the Baptism of the Holy Spirit and the instantaneous sanctification in the mid-1700's is well known. Undoubtedly, no conciliation was reached and the break-up between both positions was the conclusion as anticipated by the thinkers of the epoch. The Methodist Church was born as the fruit of this crisis, separated from the Anglican Church to the present day.

Nowadays, the Church enjoys benefits that barely two hundred years ago they did not possess. Towards the end of 1700, thousands of children roamed the streets of *Gloucester, England*, hungry, dirty and without schooling. The end of the *Victorian Era* left such a large amount of unemployed people that entire families had to go out and get a job to enable them to survive. It was in the midst of this situation when in 1785 Robert Raikes began to gather the children who roamed without a destination, on Sundays after a workweek. His objective was to utilize the Gospel as a tool for teaching and life improvement. For more than twenty-five years he raised "Sunday Schools" forming children with better life aspirations and who could know Jesus Christ as their Savior. Curiously enough, it was the Church itself, who tenaciously opposed this mission. Such a great persecution rose up against Raike's ministry, which was still in developmental stage, to the extent that a law forbidding the existence of "Sunday School" was being sought to be approved in the English Parliament. In less than the 50 years following, there were already hundreds of churches using the model created by Raikes who had reached more than 400,000 children. Nowadays, more than two hundred years later, nobody doubts that this is an effective work-tool in the modern church. Its onset was simply not effortless.

One of the most delicate points of the conflict to date is unquestionably *Biblical Eschatology*. I believe with full certainty that there is currently no other doctrinal matter having a greater number of thorny edges and varying positions. What very few believing people know is that this subject matter was not always the object of so much controversy.

The first reason I support the material written by prophetess *Ana Méndez Ferrell* is because, regardless whether her conclusions are right or wrong, is that she has dared to put on the discussion table one of the most respected "sacred cows" of the evangelical tradition.

The second is because the church that is pursuing a reformation needs to revisit "*what it believes*", and "*why*" it believes "*what*" it says it believes. **The Book of Revelation** is one of the least comprehended by modern day church and we need a new exegesis on this precious material.

The third reason is because I know the author up-close and I know she only does that which she has an absolute conviction God is telling her to do and uniquely because of this, am I led to respect her work and seriously consider it, seeking to find the revelation that perhaps for any given reason, we have not previously seen.

I am certain that if we approach this material with humility and with an openness of spirit, God will speak to us. It may not finish clearing up all the doctrinal voids about future events but it shall undoubtedly provoke some reflection, that under all points of view considered, the Church requires now more than ever.

COMMENTARY

BY
PROPHET KEVIN LEAL, PENSACOLA, FLORIDA

Elisha stood at the banks of the River Jordan with the mantle of his mentor in his hands, his memory fresh with the power he had just seen with his own eyes. He boldly exercises his faith in the God of his mentor.

"*Where is the God of Elijah?*"...fully expecting the legacy of his mentor to continue with him.

Nothing is harder to do than trying to explain the reality of a Kingdom experience someone else has not had. Even for the best of us, tradition, and the status quo often blind us to current Kingdom realities.

In her latest book, *Ana Méndez Ferrell* points us to the reality that Kingdom Living is not just in the future it is for right now.

The expression of the Kingdom in the Gospels and in the Book of Acts show us the obvious disconnects between what was considered "Kingdom normal" *then,* and "Kingdom normal" **now**.

I pray you read this book with " FRESH EYES "

SECTION 1

THE BOOK OF REVELATION SEEN FROM THE PROPHETIC PERSPECTIVE OF THE KINGDOM OF GOD

APOCALYPSE   The Revelation of Jesus Christ

Interpreting the Apocalypses, also known as the **Book of Revelation**, has been one of the greatest challenges of all times theologians have faced; if we attempt to analyze it through symbols and precise facts, we will necessarily enter the arena of speculation.

The book you are about to read is unlike anything else written regarding this precious prophetic document John left behind.

My intention is to extract the spiritual truths that will lead us to lay hold of the blessings promised to those who read it and keep its commandments.

This is a key season to understand the Apocalypse, *Book of Revelation* and God is loudly sounding off His trumpet from the heavens announcing the time to talk has arrived.

I write as a prophetess of God with the understanding that we know in part and we prophesy in part. It is not my intention to have the final word in this matter but to shed a new and different light from Heaven so you may see the **Book of Revelation** with new eyes.

In 1999 God took me to the Island of *Patmos,* where John wrote the **Book of Revelation**. During four entire days I was caught up inside the heart of the Father to see and to understand many things that He wants us to understand today.

In that dimension things are seen differently, because this is the realm where "**He is.**" So in this study I am not analyzing the **Book of Revelation** sentence by sentence, but instead I want to share with you, from The Kingdom of God perspective, the greater subjects that compose this prophecy. As we understand them, they will give us light to interpret the whole book.

Dr. Ana Méndez Ferrell

As you read through this book, it is possible that you might find things that you don't agree with at first sight. Bear with me and have patience. I will build upon each subject and your understanding will open up in a greater way.

There are things you will read that will challenge you, others that will provoke you to go deep with God, praying and inquiring. You will find concepts that will totally change the way you think about end time prophecy.

I also understand that there will be things in which your way of thinking is different from mine, and that's fine, too.

What I am completely sure about is that you will never be the same, nor will you conceive of The Kingdom of God the same way as you did when you finish reading this book.

Your Christianity will become wonderful, and you will come to know God as never before.

1 MY EXPERIENCE IN PATMOS

It was September 1999 when I arrived on the island of Patmos. God instructed me to go by myself. He had a plan and an encounter with me that would change my life forever.

The island had remained almost virgin. The port of *Skala* welcomes the tourists, but apart from this quaint little city, one can only find little fishing villages here and there. Also, atop a mountain are found the ruins of an ancient temple of Apollo and a rural road that connects everything in the island.

Since the moment of my arrival, I immediately felt the presence of God as it would have been in the time of John. It was as if time had stopped. By the sea there is a small house that the natives have preserved, and they say it was the place where the beloved disciple used to live. Next to it there is a big stone from where they say he baptized the people who dwelt on the island.

Even though John was sent as a prisoner to *Patmos,* a small population of worshipers of Diana and Apollo also inhabited the island. The island was spiritually ruled by a witch doctor called Kynops who had everybody bewitched with his great wonders.

The arrival of the Gospel of the Kingdom produced a major confrontation against the powers of the *queen of heaven* and *witchcraft,* which ended in an event that marked the history of the island.

APOCALYPSE The Revelation of Jesus Christ

It was an encounter like the one at *Mount Carmel* where Elijah faced the priests of Baal. Here is the account told by Prochorus, John's disciple:

"The sorcerer, full of pride, ridiculed St. John, who simply said, *'his power will come to an end.'*
When the crowd heard this, they beat John down and mistreated him leaving him for dead.
'Retire now,' Kynops said to the people; *'this night the dogs and eagles will devour his corpse.'* Prochorus, weeping, removed his master's body.

Suddenly at two o'clock in the morning he heard from his master's lips these words:

' *Prochorus, my son.'* *'Why, are you living, my father?'*
'Yes go and tell Myron that I am breathing still.'

Prochorus went to find Myron[1], and in giving him these tidings, both he and his family's grief turned into joy. They hastened to the spot where John was, and found him praying with his head bent towards the East. Together, they all thanked God for His deliverance.

When Kynops heard the following day that John was still alive, he gave orders to bring him before him and show John his power and to do greater marvels than those he had done the day before. The apostle was brought to the same place as the previous day.

The crowd again assembled. *'Watch me,'* Kynops said to John, and he plunged into the bay. At that moment the apostle knelt down and prayed to God while the people heard a great noise in the waters. The crowd, thinking Kynops was returning, waited

---

[1] *Myron, another of John's disciples in the island*

and watched until they grew tired; but the waves calmed again and Kynops never again returned... thus ends Prochorus's story of Kynops."²

After this amazing event, the inhabitants of *Patmos* received the Gospel and were baptized. A mosaic painting was made to commemorate this historical event.

Fig.1 - Prochorus's story of Kynops

---

² *The Island called Patmos page 147, William Edgar Geil*

A P O C A L Y P S E   The Revelation of Jesus Christ

From the moment of my arrival on the island, I had the impression that time had stopped. There was something in the air that merged with an Eternal Dimension where time does not exist. I settled in at an inexpensive but comfortable boarding house and rented a motor scooter to transport myself to wherever the Holy Spirit directed me.

The first day I went to the cave where John had received the prophecies contained in the **Book of Revelation**. It's located in the midst of a beautiful wild forest halfway up the mountain on one of the three volcanoes that form the island. Right before the cave's entrance, there is a large flat stone engraved with the scripture of *Revelation 1*:

> *I was in the Spirit on the Lord's Day, and I heard behind me a loud voice, as of a trumpet, saying, "I am the Alpha and the Omega, the First and the Last," and, "What you see, write in a book and send it to the seven churches which are in Asia: to Ephesus, to Smyrna, to Pergamos, to Thyatira, to Sardis, to Philadelphia, and to Laodicea."*

> *Then I turned to see the voice that spoke with me. And having turned I saw seven golden lampstands, and in the midst of the seven lampstands One like the Son of Man, clothed with a garment down to the feet and girded about the chest with a golden band. His head and hair were white like wool, as white as snow, and His eyes like a flame of fire; His feet were like fine brass, as if refined in a furnace, and His voice as the sound of many waters;*

Dr. Ana Méndez Ferrell

> *He had in His right hand seven stars, out of His mouth went a sharp two-edged sword, and His countenance was like the sun shining in its strength.*
>
> *And when I saw Him, I fell at His feet as dead. But He laid His right hand on me, saying to me, "Do not be afraid; I am the First and the Last. I am He who lives, and was dead, and behold, I am alive forevermore. Amen. And I have the keys of Hades and of Death.*
>
> *The Book of Revelation 1:10-18*

While I was reading this, the Holy Spirit came upon me and my eyes began watering and my body began shaking. I was standing in the very place where Jesus became manifest in His Glory and His Presence was still there. I walked slowly to the cave with a great expectation in my heart and found nobody there. It was as if the Lord had prepared it just for me.

Despite how the Greek Orthodox have defiled the cave with icons, the Presence of God was so strong that the painted images seemed like smoke with no power.

I remained there for awhile and then walked out to the forest where the hand of man had not yet destroyed the beauty of the place. I sat under the trees and entered into the Spirit as I worshipped the Lord. Little by little the atmosphere became charged with an intense presence of angels and then before my open eyes I saw the door in heaven, the same that John saw in the first century.

APOCALYPSE The Revelation of Jesus Christ

It appeared as a deep blue color in the midst of the clear summer sky. Heavenly lights shimmered around its edges. I was paralyzed in a state of ecstasy when, as clear as one can hear on Earth, I heard the trumpet voice of God saying: *"come up here!"*

At once, the Spirit caught me up as an invisible gigantic hand and I appeared 2000 years before on *Mount Calvary*, at the very moment of Christ's crucifixion. But there was something very strange for me to comprehend, it was like the apostle John and I were the same person. I saw my body and it was John's; my emotions and thoughts were no longer mine, but his. I was feeling exactly what he felt when he was seeing his Beloved hanging on the cross.

My heart was destroyed with grief, or his, I don't know, we were one and the same.

I saw Jesus hanging from the cross. All of His wounds made my own body ache. I saw His bruised deformed face and I wanted to throw myself upon Him and clean Him with kisses of love, as the blood ran down His cheeks. As He looked into my eyes, I saw that His eyes were, almost swollen shut and glassy with the look of death beginning to invade them. Even so, He looked at me and filled me with His love.

From His eyes flowed silent words that said to me, *"Thank you for being with Me in My pain. Thank you for not leaving Me alone. The Father and the Spirit have distanced Themselves because of the sin that is upon Me. Your love gives Me strength, beloved. Stay with Me until the end."*

"Yes! Yes!" my heart shouted, or John's heart. I don't know, it was like being blended together with him.

Suddenly, the body of the Lord began to tremble, and a deep distressed cry left His lips. I felt it pierce me. "*My beloved, my beloved! Don't go!*" shouted my soul, as the cry of His death resonated within me like a deafening bell. It had been imprinted on my soul, and I could not stop hearing it. The earth began to shake and the heavens darkened. There was confusion everywhere. Shouts were heard. I was paralyzed, like John. I was living everything that John lived. My eyes were fixed upon Jesus. I could not believe that my **Beloved** was there… dead.

The sound of the Roman army's armor brought me back to my senses. With violence and without any mercy whatsoever, they approached the two hanging thieves and broke their legs. But, when they came to Jesus, they saw that He was already dead so they stopped. One of the soldiers kept looking at me with disgust and then he turned away. With his spear, he pierced the heart of my Beloved. Right there in front of me, I saw Jesus' heart open and blood and water come out of his side. "*I, John, am the one giving testimony of this.*"

While I looked at the wound on His side, the Heart of Jesus changed into the Heart of the Father. Suddenly, I saw as if it were a door that opened inside this great vital organ and the Spirit took me inside. Inside was like a tabernacle having walls of flesh. There was a Courtyard, a Holy Place, and the Holy of Holies. I spent four whole days there. Each part of this impressive place was full of wounds and open lacerations. They were different and differed in severity. These are the marks of pain that remain recorded in the heart of the Father due to sin. Sin tears His insides apart in a very painful way. Inside, there were sins that affect the Courtyard, others the Holy Place, and others, where I saw the most serious wounds, went all the way into the Holy of Holies.

During the days I spent there, the Lord spoke to me about each one of His wounds. I spent a lot of time in the Holy of Holies. There the pain was the most intense. I asked the Holy Spirit what these wounds were from, what kinds of sins were so horrible that they caused this depth of damage inside the Father's heart? He told me, *"These are the sins against love in any of its forms: divisions, hatred among the brethren, slander, treason, criticism, when they attack and destroy each other, when they persecute one another filled with jealousy, when they annihilate the fallen and they hate amongst themselves. These are the sins that wound the Father the most,"* He added.

Then God showed me the impressive **Holiness of Love.** God is Love, and His Love shines with a dazzling brilliance because it is Holy. This Holiness emanates from His own Heart and is, in itself, the Holy of Holies. It was an extremely reverential Glory before me while His Love surrounded and consumed me like an intensely powerful fire that filled me in a gigantic wave of life, of grace, and of mercy. It was impressively pure, holy, infinitely HOLY. It was the Heart of God.

As this truth impressed upon my spirit, the Lord spoke to me about the Holy of Holies of His own heart. This is the place of complete, full fellowship of the deepest intimacy between God and man. It's where the fullness designed to fill our hearts finds it highest manifestation. It is there that our heart finds total and perfect union with God. It is where the Spirit of God joins with our spirit to become ONE with Him.

Then I heard a voice that came forth from the midst of the glorious holiness, and it said to me, **"My Love is holy, and there is no possibility of holiness outside of My Love."**

Holiness has nothing to do with religious conduct. It is a matter of love, of establishing ourselves upon God, of giving our lives for others as He gave His life for us. Holiness is to love from the glorious sacrifice of the Cross, where total self-denial is found so that love, which gives everything on behalf of others, can express itself. The more that we stir ourselves into that glorious essence between our spirit and His Spirit, the more I cease being "me" in order to change into "us" and loving Him through loving others, the more I am drawn near to His holiness.

Sins against love, in any of its form, touch the most delicate and sensitive area of the Heart of the Father. Love is not an option. Outside of love there is only thick darkness and it's terribly painful how we wound God. This is the commandment that Jesus gave us to keep:

> *"A new commandment I give to you, that you love one another; as I have loved you, that you also love one another.*
> *By this all will know that you are My disciples, if you have love for one another."*
>
> *John 13:34 -35*

Can a lost world, so needy of love, a world that cries in its loneliness and its deepest emptiness, see us as Christ's disciples when there is so much selfishness, so much division, so much judging and criticizing one other? Will we have the courage to see Truth and cry out to understand the highest concept of the universe, which is the *Love of God*, greater and deeper than anyone can imagine?

A P O C A L Y P S E   The Revelation of Jesus Christ

Revelation is found in the Light, and Light flows out from His Love, the more the love, the more the revelation.

In some of my books I have written about the many different aspects of my experience within the heart of God[3] as the topic demanded it. But what I saw and understood behind that heavenly door requires many more books, and this is one of them.

God allowed me to see His Throne, His Court of Righteousness and the myriads of angels that work together along with The Lord and the Church. In Heaven both dimensions are united. When we worship or intercede we become visible in the heavenly realm. Millions of tongues and nations emerge before the throne and are bathed in His Grace and Favor. Jesus Himself is the Heavenly City from where the River of Living Water flows to nourish us and to give us life.

I stood in the very stage of the **Book of Revelation**, the most powerful revelation of Jesus as the King of Kings and also the manual He gave us to rule and reign with Him. It's in this revelation of the prophetic dimensions where we can know Him with an unveiled face, where we are introduced to understand the mysteries of His Kingdom.

---

[3] *"Seated in Heavenly Places" & "Eat My Flesh, Drink My Blood", both by Ana Méndez Ferrell.*

2 THE DILEMMA OF INTERPRETATION

1. The Times We Live In

What times am I living in? What is God expecting of me and of this generation I am a part of? What am I doing in this world, are all basic questions, answered, based on what we have determined to believe concerning the End Times.

What we believe, to this regard, fashions us and constrains us to make vital decisions. If everything will end in the upcoming years, then logically I will plan my life on a short-term basis. On the other hand, if this isn't so, then I will plan on leaving an inheritance for my children and my grandchildren.

If I believe Jesus will reign with His saints only after His Second Coming, then I will aspire to have the blessings of His Kingdom then. But if I believe that His Kingdom is already in the midst of us and that He is already ruling with His saints, then NOW is when I will do whatever it takes to grab a hold of what this implies.

Gaining full clarity and truth regarding this matter determines my purpose and my lifestyle therefore this becomes imperatively important. This fixates our aim on whether we can receive from God today, or if we should only live in expectation of the future without really receiving anything while we are in this life.

I reached the conclusion that if my life and my destiny depended on my understanding of Eschatology, then seeking the Truth in the Bible and going deeper with God until He gives me the answers that I am looking for, is very important to me and is also my responsibility. This is also my exhortation for all of those who are seeking His truth.

Nowadays we find ourselves amidst a wave of terror that is being unleashed regarding the approaching "end of the world." We hear everywhere that the Earth will be destroyed some talk about the rapture of the Church while others think it is a mistaken interpretation of Scripture. At the end, the world sinks into doubt and fear while the Church struggles to understand Truth; some based on traditional teachings while others believe what God is showing the prophets of today. After my experience in *Patmos,* much of what I had thought to be true, because of what I had been taught, changed completely. To see the truths of the **Book of Revelation** from the heavenly perspective changed my life and my way of reading this Book.

I clearly understand that every revelation needs to be confirmed by the Bible. Therefore I have spent years praying about these impressive truths I saw and experienced in the dimensions of The Kingdom of God, as to whether they were certain in the Word.

As a prophetess of God, I have sought the answers to these questions for almost 12 years of studying and receiving revelation. I sense a deep responsibility over this generation God has called me to touch. I desire to give them what I consider God has given to me for them. The **Book of Revelation** is undoubtedly the most important book regarding this subject and the one I consider to be the most misinterpreted in our days.

God wants to open our understanding so we can grasp His designs, His ways, and His thoughts.

This is why I am asking you to read this book with a humble and open spirit so you can understand things that will surely shake much of your theology regarding Eschatology.[4]

I also encourage you to pray, seek and ask the Lord to reveal to you as His child, His divine truth; to question yourself, why do you believe what you believe about these subjects and if necessary, make certain adjustments.

> *Then said he unto me, Fear not, Daniel: for from the first day that thou didst set thine heart to understand, and to chasten thyself before thy God, thy words were heard, and I am come for thy words.*
> *Daniel 10:12*

God loves to reveal Himself to a humble, willing heart and to take him or her to the depths of His Knowledge and His Revelation.

The Lord does not want to leave us at the level we are in. He wants to take us to the measure of the stature of the perfect man which is Christ Jesus; He wants us to enter the fullness of the Glory He has reserved for us. Many things that can be shaken must be shaken for this to happen, and in this way, that which is immortal becomes manifest.

---

[4] *Eschatology is defined as the study of the final events in Scripture. This science not only determines the things that will happen, but also our view of the present day world, it will mold us and give substance to our thoughts.*

> *Whose voice then shook the earth: but now he hath promised, saying, Yet once more I shake not the earth only, but also heaven. And this word, Yet once more, signifieth the removing of those things that are shaken, as of things that are made, that those things which cannot be shaken may remain.*
>
> *Hebrews 12:26, 27*

2. OT Interpretation Of The *Book Of Revelation*

Many books written on this subject are based on the interpretation of symbols and based on the preconceived ideas of the destruction of the Earth. This is because the meaning of the word *"apocalypses"* is totally distorted in the dictionaries of many languages, English and Spanish among them.

Words carry concepts and ideologies that lead us to think in a certain manner and connect us to certain areas of the brain.

For example, if I hear the word *"beauty"* I will necessarily think about something pleasant and I will tune into that part of my brain where I perceive joy and happiness. If on the contrary I hear the word *"abortion"* I will think about death, destruction, something that never succeeds and this will activate the pain center in the brain.

The word *"Apocalypses"* (**apokalupsis**) is a Greek word which means *revelation, apparition, coming, illumination, manifestation, bring to the light.*[5]

---

[5] *Strong Concordance 602., ap-ok-al´-oop-sis; from 601; disclosure: — appearing, coming, lighten, manifestation, be revealed, revelation.*

Dr. Ana Méndez Ferrell

Dictionaries however translate it as: *a great disaster, a sudden and very bad event that causes much fear, loss, or destruction*[6]

In English it is interpreted as: *monumental catastrophe, total destruction, extinction, annihilation, death.*[7]

Whether we like it or not, these incorrect definitions have conditioned our minds to interpret the **Book of Revelation** as a book of destruction, death and the end of all created things.

This has produced an *end of the world* concept in every culture. In every millennium and at every turn of the century the nations expect the world's final moment.

Whether God will destroy the Earth or not is almost impossible to discern, given the manner in which the consciousness of the world has conceived the tremendous grand finale.

What if God loves the Earth and the work of His hands and does not want to destroy it? Who is going to believe Him and come against such a forceful flow of mainstream thinking?

If on the contrary, the **Book of Revelation** was, as its name indicates, a book of the revelation of lightand of divine manifestation?

How are we able to read it in this manner if the rest of the world wants to view it as something terrible?

---

[6] *Mirriam Webster Dictionary,* http://www.merriam-webster.com/dictionary/apocalypse
[7] *Oxford American Writer's Thesaurus*

The prophetic ministry has only been recognized as such in the last 30 to 40 years, by a few. If the **Book of Revelation** was analyzed by wise men who didn't have in them the Spirit of Prophecy, this would have caused great interpretation errors. In many of these cases, scholars have been reproducing what was taught to them from generation to generation without even questioning where these theologies came from.

I have understood that the only way to genuinely hear God regarding anything is finding a totally neutral position. Massive mainstream thinking can lead us to err.

In 1999 when I was in the island of *Patmos,* I was led to comprehend many things about this book. The fruit of those days opened my understanding to many truths. One of these truths has taken more than 12 years to begin unfurling and continues to grow inside of me the revelation of the book of "***Apocalypses***", or **Book of Revelation,** I write about here.

3. How The *Book Of Revelation* Was Written

The first thing I realized at the island, and based on serious research, was that John wrote this book during various sittings.

He frequently went to the cave on the top of the hill bringing with him one of his disciples named *Prochorus*[8] who would write the visions as John narrated them from the heavenly dimension.

---

[8] *Historical fact documented in the Island of Patmos.*

Fig. 2 - Apostle John receiving the revelation of the Apocalypse, while it is written by his disciple Prochorus

As one enters this realm, one doesn't loose consciousness and it is possible to talk about what is being seen without coming back from the experience. The spirits of the prophets are subject to the prophets (*1 Corinthians 14:32*)!

4. The Order Of The Canon

When John's writings were discovered, they were not in order and when the Canon of the New Testament was put together, these writing were accommodated as best they saw fit. This is why we find passages that apparently are in conflict with one another if we try to study this book from a chronological point of view. Some talk about a total destruction of the Universe when the sixth seal is opened and then at the end of Chapter 22 there's a call to come to salvation. Chapter 20 talks about a Final Judgment and in the 22nd Chapter we read about people being called to come to Christ for salvation. We also read about those who try to enter the city but cannot.

It is logical to suppose that after *THE* Final Judgment there will be no more room for the preaching of the Gospel and neither a place for those who are trying to force their way into the city,

We see yet another contradiction within the traditional chronological interpretation when *Babylon* falls in Chapter 11, then it falls again in Chapter 17, but its sentence is handed down in Chapter 18. We then see the *Great Day of Wrath* falling upon the Earth and the sky rolling up as a scroll in Chapter 6 and yet in the 14th chapter the angel goes out to preach the Gospel.

If we put Chapters 21 and 22 after the Judgment we will never understand what Jesus already did for us in His First Coming and this is an absolute tragedy.

On the other hand, when the Bible Canon was put together in the fourth century, it was decided to put this ***Book of Revelation*** at the end. Like it or not, this order, psychologically compels us to view it as the Book of "The End." If they had placed it after the Gospels, then maybe we would view it as truly the Kingdom Book Jesus left us. And, if they had placed the Book of the Acts of the Apostles at the end, maybe the Church would still be full of life doing greater works than Jesus did, as He declared it.

3. THE ESSENCE OF THE BOOK OF REVELATION

1. The Book's Main Subject: THE REVELATION OF CHRIST

Heaven is timeless. God is the great I AM, the *Continuous Present*. In Heaven we can travel to the past in an instant and in the next be transferred to thousands of years into the future. Although there is no time in Heaven it is not static either, it is impressively alive and active.

The book was written using a heavenly language and symbols that are not from Earth. It's The Kingdom of God's manual and legacy so we can govern with Jesus. The central theme in the ***Book of Revelation*** is "**The Revelation of Jesus Christ**". This is the name of the book and also its content.

> ***The Revelation of Jesus Christ,*** *which God gave unto Him to show unto His servants things which must shortly come to pass. And He sent and signified it by His angel unto His servant John,*
>
> *Revelation 1:1*

It's not a book about the end of the world; it's a book on **how to know Jesus in His Glory and about His Government.** It's a book that is alive in the *Eternal Present* of God.

APOCALYPSE The Revelation of Jesus Christ

It's a book on Government and about Heavenly Understanding. The Old Testament teaches us how God The Father reigned over the Earth while it was in a fallen state. The Father announces the things that will happen through the coming of His Son. The Ancient Covenant teaches us the character of the Father and His dealings with men through His people Israel.

The ***Book of Revelation*** is the government of the New Heaven and the New Earth, which have been redeemed by Messiah; it's the reign of Christ after He united Heaven and Earth in Him.

> *He hath made known unto us the mystery of His will, according to His good pleasure which He hath purposed in Himself, that in the dispensation of the fullness of times He might **gather together in one all things in Christ, both which are in heaven and which are on earth**, even in Him.*
>
> *Ephesians 1:9-10*

It's the only book where God promises a blessing upon reading it because it is a book that teaches us how to live in the revelation of Christ in His Eternity; it's the victory of His Kingdom imparting the most important tools for the saints to rule and judge together with Him.

It's not an obsolete book as some people assume, nor is it an unfulfilled book as others think. It contains something powerful regarding the revealed Glory of Christ reserved for those who read it.

> *Blessed is he that readeth, and they that hear the words of this prophecy, and keep those things which are written therein; for the time is at hand.*
>
> *Revelation 1:3*

What blessedness could there be in reading this prophecy if it doesn't bring any life application for us now or for every believer throughout the ages?

2. Jesus must be revealed to every believer

This is the revelation God gave John, but God reveals Himself to each one of us in a unique and singular manner according to our call and our position in the Kingdom.

The Church needs to be grounded in "the revelation of Jesus Christ" as Jesus told His disciples when He would ask them who did they say He was.

> *And Jesus answered and said unto him, "Blessed art thou, Simon Bar-Jonah, for flesh and blood hath not revealed it unto thee, but My Father who is in Heaven. And I say also unto thee, that thou art Peter, and upon this rock I will build My church; and the gates of hell shall not prevail against it.*
>
> *Matthew 16:17-18*

The revelation of Christ directly given by the Holy Spirit is what lays the foundation for a Church that cannot be shaken by the gates of hell; this is what the **Book of Revelation** is all about.

Jesus Christ reveals Himself to John to give us the keys of His Kingdom and trains us to rule and to destroy the gates of hell.

3. The Purposes of the Book

a) This is the Book of the Testimony of Jesus and the Realm of the Spirit

This is the most marvelous manual on the prophetic dimension, which is the testimony of Jesus. It's the revelation of the original blueprint from where all things were created. All the temple designs and its ordinances in the Ancient Covenant were only a type and shadow of the true ones in Heaven. This is the Book about the identity of Jesus as the sovereign King of the Universe.

b) Victory Against Our Enemies

The essence of this book is the Glory of Christ revealed to topple the structures of *Babylon*, which are the foundation of the devil's government.

This is a book that teaches us to defeat the enemy, to judge and to legislate in the dimensions of the Spirit, to change the destiny of our nations so these turn to God.

It teaches us how God judges from His throne and the diverse manners He does it, not as something that is accomplished on one single occasion but the manner and the instruments He uses to judge.

To reign means, among other things, to establish Righteousness. This is what a righteous King does and we have been called to take The Kingdom of God and His Righteousness throughout the Earth.

c) It Reveals Who We Are In Christ

It tells us who we are in Christ as priests and kings; what it means to be the **Tabernacle of God on Earth**, the *Jerusalem* from above, the *New Jerusalem* manifested in the temple not made with human hands but an Eternal One in the heavens and alive among the believers. In it, we understand the wonder of being married to Him not in the future but NOW.

d) It Shows Us the True Structure of the Church

It's a book that talks to us about the design of God regarding His Church, its form, its structure which is a cube and not a pyramid, along with its great power.

It teaches us to recognize how the structures of this world have been designed and how to destroy them to obtain the victory.

e) It Produces a Grandiose Fruit

It's a book that will mightily change your life, your destiny and the manner in which you perceive your Christianity.

To interpret it will require you to understand certain basic principles regarding the Thinking and the Heart of God. I will begin expounding on these foundational issues so light is shed for us to see the mysteries hidden in this marvelous book. To attempt to discern it based on words, symbols, analogies, or chronologies will only lead us to error since it is a heavenly book written from the Spirit of God in a spiritual language to the Spirit of His Church.

4. The Apocalypses: The Kingdom Manual

a). Kings and Priests

The ***Book of Revelation*** is our Kingdom Manual to govern jointly with Jesus. As we previously said, it is not a prophecy about the end of the world but the revelation of Jesus Christ in His Glory. It is a heavenly book designed to let us know about the dimensions of Heaven and its operation on Earth. **The Church was born prophetic to be the voice of God and to reveal Him to the world.**

Jesus already ascended to the Throne and sent His angel to John to instruct him about His government and how He would rule together with His saints and to let him know about the Church's glorious power.

From the beginning of the ***Book of Revelation***, Jesus introduces Himself as Sovereign over the kings of the Earth and announces to us our heavenly rank as *kings and priests*. It's a message to be understood with a kingdom mentality.

> *… and from Jesus Christ, who is the faithful witness, and the first-begotten of the dead, and the **(sovereign) prince over the kings of the earth**. Unto Him that loved us, and washed us from our sins in His own blood, and hath made us **kings and priests** unto God and His Father, to Him be glory and dominion forever and ever. Amen.*
>
> *Revelation 1:5-6*

He wants to train us to reign and to be priests unto His Father. The first lesson is that Jesus, before being crowned King had to be a Priest. This is the Mediator between God and man, the One who ministers and makes The Heavenly Father tangible and visible. He brings the truths and the essence of Heaven and manifests them in our midst. A priest is he who sacrifices unto the Lord. Jesus was the ultimate sacrificer through His death at The Cross. He is the faithful witness because He reproduces in a reliable manner everything the Father does and speaks.

Jesus is the High Priest of the good things of the coming Age, which are the New Earth and the New Heavens.

> *But Christ, having come a High Priest of good things to come, by a greater and more perfect tabernacle, not made with hands (that is to say, not of this building),*
> *Hebrews 9:11*

He did not minister the earthly things as the priests of the Old Covenant did, but the heavenly ones that were about to come to Earth.

He was then exalted in glory to reign in the Tabernacle not made by human hands but the Eternal one in the heavens.

In like manner we have to understand **our mission of manifesting the Father** so the world can be reconciled to Him. This will depend on whether or not Christ is revealed in our hearts and this is what gives us authority to have the same dominion Adam had.

It's the Revelation of Christ that gives us access to the keys of the kingdom and lays the foundation so the gates of *hades* do not prevail against us. *(Matthew 16:17-19)*

The **Book of Revelation** is the revelation God gave to John, but God has one for each one of us who will manifest the message with the tools we need to exercise our service as kings.

For this to happen we need to learn to "be in the Spirit" just like John, since our kingdom is from the spiritual spheres.

I was in the Spirit on the Lord's Day, and I heard behind me a great voice as of a trumpet,
Revelation 1:10

John was trained to hear the voice of God and knew that if he was able to hear Him then he could also see Him. He heard Him from his spirit with great expectation, knowing that Jesus continually manifested unto him.

He was "in the Spirit" on the Lord's Day. When we enter in Him, we are introduced into the Great "I Am", in the *Continuous Present* of the Presence of God. In there, time ceases to exist, past and future.

We enter into the Eternal of His Being on the Lord's Day, a place where there is no time. Therefore when John says I was on the *Lord's Day* he wanted to say he was on God's time, inside the realm where He IS and where He manifests Himself.

The Spirit of Prophecy is the testimony of Jesus. **The *Book of Revelation* is the Testimony of Jesus.** For this reason it cannot be interpreted from the mindset of Earth, it can only be interpreted from being inside of Him: "I was **In** the Spirit", that's how this book was written, entering the spiritual dimension of Heaven, into God's realm.

Likewise when we learn to be **IN** His Spirit, His Power is revealed to us to be born and live in the sphere of His dominion.

I   It's the individual revelation of Christ in His Glory that gives authority to the Church

When the Father revealed the identity of the Christ to Simon Peter it led him to possess the keys of the Kingdom. Jesus talks about the same thing to John in the ***Book of Revelation***. He displays Himself to him as holding the keys of *death* and *hades*. Therefore, the vivid revelation of Christ in your life will give you the keys to govern.

Upon his return from *Patmos,* John confronted the powers of Diana of the Ephesians and the temple of the goddess crumbled down. While at the island, he also defied the power of Kynops as we mentioned before.

The revelation of Jesus in His Glory makes John fall as dead *(Revelation 1:17)*. It takes a lot of hard work for many people to die to their flesh and to the world because Jesus has never been revealed to them in this manner. The truth is that when this happens to you the Radiance and Love that emanate from Him is such that you want nothing else of this world, you remain marked forever.

You have to see Him in all His Glory, living and reigning inside of you, fusing with your spirit and becoming ONE with you. Only by dying to your flesh will you be able to see Him in the right proportion of Who He is in your life.

Everything He needs to do, is to captivate every part of your being. You have to see Him in all His majesty until you fall to the ground as Peter did during the miraculous fishing and tell Him: *stay away from me for I am a sinner.* It's in this position that Jesus can teach you to be a king without the danger of your becoming proud.

It's in this position from where He reveals the whole dimension of His Kingdom. Heaven cannot be interpreted; it has to reveal itself to us. Therein lies the difference to know the truths in the ***Book of Revelation***. The ***Book of Revelation*** is based on the Old Testamentarian prophecy revealed from Heaven by the same Spirit of prophecy, which is Jesus, who is the steadfast anchor of our understanding.

4 THE POWER OF PRECONCEIVED IDEAS

At the time Jesus came to Earth, the Scribes as well as the Doctors of the Law and Priests were all learned men in the Law yet failed to recognize the coming of Messiah. The reason was that they had studied the Scriptures so much that they had set their preconceived ideas over and above God's revelation, and even though they had the Son of God in front of them, they failed to see Him as such.

Their idea of Messiah coming in a chariot of fire from Heaven just as Elijah had left was so deeply rooted in their minds that when He was born in a stable (a Succoth tent) in *Bethlehem*, son of a carpenter, it became impossible for them to believe it. This simply did not fit with their theologies. A child conceived by a virgin out of wedlock? What matter of insanity was this! They were expecting a King coming in a chariot who would defeat the Romans and would sit on the throne of David here in the earthly *Jerusalem*.

But this Jesus had not come to sit on a throne of this world. His kingdom was not of this world. They were confused; they wanted a kingdom here at all costs not at an unknown dimension.

> *Therefore Pilate entered again into the Praetorium, and summoned Jesus and said to Him, "Are You the King of the Jews?" Jesus*

*answered, "My kingdom is not of this world. If My kingdom were of this world, then My servants would be fighting so that I would not be handed over to the Jews; but as it is, **My kingdom is not of this realm."***

Therefore Pilate said to Him, "So You are a king?" Jesus answered, "You say correctly that I am a king. For this I have been born, and for this I have come into the world, to testify to the truth. Everyone who is of the truth hears My voice."

John 18:33, 36, 37

Having been questioned by the Pharisees as to when the kingdom of God was coming: He answered them and said, "The kingdom of God is not coming in a visible form, Nor will they say, 'Look, here it is!' or, 'There it is!' ***For behold, the kingdom of God is in your midst."***

Luke 17:20-21 Literal Translation

They couldn't stand this truth! According to them, the Messiah that was to come was a king that would save them and reign on David's physical throne. They couldn't conceive of an invisible kingdom and therefore they crucified him.

This compels me to think carefully: why did the theologians in Israel, who back then were great scholars, meticulous with the use of commas and titles, missed it?

A four thousand year old scriptural legacy tradition failed them for the discerning of the prophecy. Why? Because they had it all figured out ahead of time and when God did things according to His way and not theirs they couldn't change their way of thinking.

God had to resort to some gentile magicians from the East, to shepherd boys who were keeping the night watch and to Joseph and Mary's few close friends and relatives. These were not great theologians, scribes or doctors but simple people who would believe when they saw the heavens open and the angels talking to them (Luke 2:8-14).

God always seeks the simple-hearted, those who are capable of changing their paradigms when He reveals Himself; those who acknowledge before Him that they do not know all things. And if God is taking us from light to light and from glory to glory, necessarily there will be things that will be revealed to us in a different manner from what we used to believe and we need to have the spiritual ability to make the adjustments.

1. Jesus Opens Our Understanding

The Scribes and the Doctors of the Law were not the only ones who failed to understand the Scriptures; it got to a point that even Jesus' disciples ran into the wall and had no understanding either.

After living with Him during three years and seeing all His wonders, Jesus had to open their understanding so they could understand the Scriptures. The time they spent with Him and were discipled and trained did not enable them to understand the Scriptures.

After His resurrection, Jesus appeared to two of his disciples on the road to *Emaus* and from there they headed to where the others had gathered. None recognized Him in His incorruptible body until He parted the bread and their eyes were opened.

> *And He said unto them, "These are the words which I spoke unto you while I was yet with you, that all things must be fulfilled which were written in the Law of Moses and in the Prophets and in the Psalms concerning Me." Then opened He their understanding*, **that they might understand the Scriptures,**
>
> *Luke 24:44-45*

We see two impressive things here. The first one is His opening of their understanding to understand Scripture, and the second is He reveals how EVERYTHING THAT WAS WRITTEN ABOUT HIM IN THE TORAH, IN PSALMS AND THE PROPHETS HAD BEEN FULFILLED.

In English it's hard to grasp because the auxiliary verb "*must*" is the same in present, future and in past tense, yet in the original Greek and in other translations from other languages it says, "… had been fulfilled"

It is important to understand that Jesus, as the Messiah of Israel, came to fulfill everything that was writen. Jesus in the flesh is the end of the Old Covenant.

He is the fulfillment of all righteousness and of all the Law. His earthly ministry was only to the Jews, not to the Gentiles. Matthew, Mark, Luke, and John are the end of the Old Testament and not the beginning of the New.

That is why we see Jesus constantly saying in the gospels, "*I am doing this so the Scripture be fulfilled,*" and "*I am saying this so the Scripture is fulfilled.*"

Dr. Ana Méndez Ferrell

The New Testament should start in Acts 10 when Cornelius, the first Gentile, received the Gospel. The prophecies that Jesus spoke, that would come to pass, were given to the Jews of His time, who were His assignment.

If we separate Jesus from the fulfillment of the Old Testament, we are not recognizing Him as the Messiah of Israel and we are actually separating Christianity from Judaism.

If we read the Gospels as the fulfillment of all Scripture, then we will see the finished work of Christ. If we read it as the New Testament, then He did not finished His work and we need to wait for Him to do it.

> *I have glorified You on the earth. I have finished the work which You have given Me to do.*
> *John 17:4*

Unfortunately when the Canon was made four centuries after Christ, they decided that the Old Testament finished in Malachi, and the New Testament should start in Matthew, when Jesus was born. This separates the people of Israel from their Messiah. This is a great fundamental mistake that we need to consider if we want to interpret what Jesus prophesied and to whom He spoke this to.

These two truths are relevant to the subjects we are touching on. Unless Jesus opens our understanding to understand Scripture we will find ourselves in the same condition as the Scribes, the Doctors of the Law and Jesus' disciples.

Jesus holds in Himself the perfect interpretation of Scripture and He tells us that everything pertaining to Him has already been fulfilled. Using passages from Isaiah, Daniel and Zechariah saying there are certain things not yet fulfilled is a doctrinal error.

Just as Jesus' disciples hit a wall that wouldn't allow them to understand Scripture, we may likewise find ourselves in this same situation.

> *Blessed are the pure in heart, for they shall see God.*
> *Matthew 5:8*

I feel that there is nothing more dangerous than to cling to a prophetic interpretation and say, "This is how it is and I am not budging."

What makes us think that we are incapable of being wrong when the great Scribes and Doctors of the Law failed so miserably?

They were sincerely mistaken yet their theologies and preconceived ideas were more important to them than God Himself.

I ask you to pray at this moment for Jesus Christ Himself to open your understanding to perceive the Scripture in the **Book of Revelation** as He alone can reveal it unto you.

Ask Him for eyes to see what you couldn't see before, and ears to hear His Spirit clearly.

Through this book we will find out what the reality of the Kingdom is and we will analyze many Scriptural passages that will fill us with light to understand what Jesus did in His First Coming.

The Holy Spirit will change our manner of thinking so we may be used as the kings and priests we represent for God the Father, seeing the inheritance of light and revelation in the **Apocalypses, the Book of Revelation**. Then, we will fill the Earth with the knowledge of the Glory of God as the waters cover the sea.

5 THE TWO GREAT ERAS

1. Patmos, Second Vision

I found myself inside the Holy of Holies of God's heart, the place from where life and the greatest love of the entire Universe flows. The Holiness of Love shone with such brilliance, it pierced me and sanctified me at the same time. Everything that is within me became holy in that place because no uncleanliness can remain there.

I was moved by a combination of pain and joy. On one end I saw His wounds caused by each one of us and on the other end, the love that would exude from that place, which far from blaming me, attracted me to Him to sanctify me and to love me. My spirit, which I was able to see in that place, was filled with a light that enabled me to know many things at the same time. I could see towards different directions and I could see many doors but not like those on Earth, they were placed on different planes and each one led to a different dimension.

Around God's heart were the doors that came from the sufferings of Christ. Every drop of blood shed and each wound born into His flesh formed a door. It's impossible to enter into each one of these during a human being's lifetime, but those who are granted to enter lead to marvelous places of His Wisdom, His Intelligence, His Power, His Riches and His Glory.

APOCALYPSE The Revelation of Jesus Christ

Heaven is multidimensional; it's not like Earth where all we see with our natural eyes is the visible realm. There is no up or down, no before or after, everything simply "is" in each one of the infinite dimensions and manifestations of God.

In Heaven everything is agile, light, weightless, and spacious. There is no way to describe the beauty seen in the dimensions of light. The Holy Spirit attracted my attention to one of the doors on one of those flesh-like walls that composed the most sensitive parts of His heart. More than a door, it was like a large gash whose edges were ripped open. I approached it and a severely intense pain filled me to my innards. *"Enter"* said the Lord. I had barely set foot when I was transported to a very different place, atop a high mountain from where the Garden of Eden could be seen.

It was the moment right before the fall.

Everything was full of the love of God and He rejoiced in loving His family, the children He had created. He made them out of the same love substance that flows from His Holy Of Holies. They were just like Him in the terrestrial domain. Suddenly, everything began to vibrate in a strange manner and a black shadow entered Eden and took the form of a serpent. The dialogue of death ensued which produced the fall, and then silence fell. A deep hollow akin to a black hole in space formed around Adam and his wife. Then came a frightful thundering from Heaven and an intense outcry of pain paralyzed the universe. I turned to see where that terrible sound came from and instantly I saw how the Father's heart was being rent. He had lost his beloved children His dearest family in an instant. It's difficult to describe such a pain. Only when we have loved with all our hearts and lose the one we love, can we feel a fragment of what the Father felt. There was silence for a long time. Everything was like arrested in an uncontrollable pain. No angel dared to move.

The whole Earth became covered with deep darkness and the pain of death and separation enshrouded the Earth's surface, while a deep chasm isolated it from the heavens. Man ended up condemned to a life in the shadows of death and darkness. Sheol had opened its mouth and sickness, distress, poverty, hate, hopelessness, sadness and evil filled the world. The terror of death had taken over the hearts of humanity.

Seen from Heaven, the Earth resembled a parched land covered by thorns. Deep darkness seeped from hell and enabled it to prevail producing an unquenchable thirst in all men. The denseness of the deep darkness covering the Earth could be seen and felt. The frequency of the land was heavy; the sound was grave and strident, chaotic like the roar of frightened wild animals. That density can never penetrate the acute lightness of Heaven's frequency.

I cried as I felt the pain of death in God's heart throughout my body. But something happened that moved me to happiness. From that same torn heart I saw a light come forth. It was the light of Jesus, the love that never ceases to be; the Spirit of Prophecy that was coming from Heaven announcing the marvelous plan of Salvation. The light began taking form before my eyes. It became a great mountain from where milk and honey began to flow, and from here, also new wine flowed having such a fragrance that it filled the whole place. A beautiful fountain of clear waters shimmering with lights as stars navigating amidst it, opened up; there were also tongues of fire dancing over them. I witnessed how rivers formed and streamed downwards and became a great river that flooded an enormous valley.

APOCALYPSE The Revelation of Jesus Christ

I then saw other mountains being fashioned from the great mountain; waters of life, honey and new wine flowed from each one and filled the Heaven as far as my eyes could see.[9] All of these joined to the great mountain were Jesus, but as I saw this, He still had not descended to Earth, which remained parched, and in pain.

I remained there gazing for a long time. I don't know how long since there is no time in Heaven and a moment in my consciousness can equal millenniums up there. At that moment, an elderly man appeared next to me; his face was beaming and his garments were wine red. I knew he was one of the 24 elders that are before the throne. He gave me a key and told me: "*This is the key of knowledge.*" When I held it in my hands I felt a very strong unction that encased me, and my eyes were filled with light. I could see various dimensions at the same time without moving anywhere.

I then saw how other type of heavens were formed, between the Earth, and God's Heaven. These heavens were of deep darkness and a great city began forming within it resembling a gigantic beast full of internal structures. It had tentacles that appeared as pipeline-encased roadways that led to thousands of cities of darkness that received nourishment from the mother city.

There were also diverse dimensions and doors in those heavens that led some to Earth, and others to the depths of hell. Seven mountains also surrounded the city, all of them sinister-looking, craggy and parched. They were filled with caves that led to thousands of prisons. Both the cities and the mounts were teeming with demons and there were thrones over the summits of these mountains. These were covered by structures resembling transparent vaults that protected them so no one could tear them down.

---

[9] Words that confirm this vision : *Joel 3:18 and Zechariah 13:1*

I was still looking at all of this when there came a great music from Heaven, like myriads of angels together with the majestic sound from the wings of the cherubim that resounded in all the celestial Universe. Following the music, thunder and lightning were heard and the whole sky was clouded with the Presence of the Most High. A resplendent light began to whirl inside the cloud becoming more and more magnificent until it took a form and turned into a human fetus. He began to grow inside a woman, it was Mary's womb. In the Spirit He appeared full of light surrounded by water and blood and a rainbow enveloped him. He was born and became a child, then a man.

I was seeing in the heavens the moment Jesus became flesh and then lived among us. Time is no more in that place and everything appears to occur in instants. Blood enveloped Him completely and He began to be condensed as a liquid cloud until He transformed into the perfect cornerstone rock that gleamed as a diaphanous and extremely luminous diamond, which remained floating in the middle of the Universe. It was like seeing the crucifixion from another dimension, from the place where the power of His blood transformed into His very own Glory.

From this rock came an explosion and its shock waves covered the heavens with light as when a star forms. I then saw one resembling the Son of Man in the midst of the diamond and seated in a Throne full of Glory. His Glory covered the Earth and it was filled with His Praise; from the Throne a voice came saying: *"It is done."* Jesus was now seated at the right hand of His Father, on His Throne.

This was the heavenly vision God gave me, of what happened in one of the heavenly dimensions, when Jesus came to the Earth and then ascended back to His Father. This fact changed everything in the Universe. The Earth once again was filled with the Presence of God. Heaven and Earth once again were united in Jesus.[10]

The first heavens passed away. These were the heavens where the Throne of Redemption had not yet been occupied. The former Earth also passed away, the Earth of deep darkness, death and pain. Everything was filled with Jesus, with His Light. I then saw a New Earth and a New Heaven. It was the same Earth, the beautiful planet God made and loved but now it was filled with His Glory, with His Presence. A crystalline coating of the blood of Jesus was wrapped around it and the Holy Spirit filled it with His Luminosity, with His Wisdom making the Father accessible to all who seek Him.

The Holy Mountain with its springs of waters was established over the Earth to all who want to drink from it. Its rainbow shines forever, uniting Heaven and Earth, which shall never again be destroyed. The Earth is no longer the old Earth covered by darkness, dryness and without hope. It's a new Earth and a new Heaven because the Righteousness bought for us at the price of the Cross now dwells in it. Jesus, the promised Messiah became flesh and came to Earth, and changed the Heavens and changed the Earth forever and His Kingdom shall never end.

Everything has been done, but some things need to be manifested from the invisible to the visible. As His righteousness and His justice become established through a generation of true sons of God, we will see a better Earth, with the glory that we all expect to see. The divine design of His magnificent city will also be seen in every city that converts to Jesus the King of Kings.

---

[10] *He that descended is the same who also ascended up far above all heavens, that He might fill all things - Ephesians 4:10*

He will soon bring judgments that will destroy the wicked and will reward the true righteous. People will come to know God and the Earth will be filled with knowledge of the Glory of God as the waters cover the sea.

2. The Key Of Understanding

This vision, along with receiving the key of understanding that is given to all who want to know Jesus and seek to walk in His Kingdom, changed my way of reading Scripture. As I mentioned in the previous chapter of this book, Jesus told His disciples that everything that had been written about Him, in the Law of Moses, the Psalms and the Prophets has already been fulfilled. Jesus is THE SPIRIT OF PROPHECY, *(Revelation 19:10)* and He is the One who spoke through all His prophets.

> *Of which salvation the prophets have enquired and searched diligently, who prophesied of the grace that should come unto you:*
>
> *Searching what, or what manner of time **the Spirit of Christ which was in them** did signify, when it testified beforehand the sufferings of Christ, and the glory that should follow.*
>
> *1 Peter 1:10-11*

If He said everything had been fulfilled, then this is the anchor of Revelation and Interpretation.

A) The Plan of God

To know what was the mind of God throughout His entire plan of salvation is critical to interpret the Scriptures.

APOCALYPSE The Revelation of Jesus Christ

The Bible is divided into two great sections, which clearly marks out two eras and two distinct covenants of God's dealings with men.

Since the fall of Adam, the scriptures announce the coming of the Messiah as the solution to the deep darkness that had settled in to reign over the Earth.

The Father had **one single redeeming Plan** with His Son, the Messiah through whom He would restore all things to their original state in the *Garden of Eden*. God created man to rule and to have dominion on Earth through fellowship with his Creator and this is what Jesus came to restore.

His redeeming work concluded at the Cross of Calvary. He clearly stated: "*It is finished.*" The Kingdom of God was established when Jesus ascended to the Heavens and sat at the right hand of the Father to reign together with His Body which is the Church.

> *To him that overcometh, will I grant to sit with Me on My throne, even as I also overcame and am set down with My Father on **His throne**.*
> *Revelation 3:21*

This Plan of Redemption is announced throughout the entire history in the Old Testament. This was to bring a new phase, a new century, a new era full of God where His designs were to be established.

The Messiah would bring about the Glory that Adam once lost and it would manifest again in the sons and daughters of God.

Dr. Ana Méndez Ferrell

Arise, shine, for thy light is come, and the glory of the LORD is risen upon thee. For behold, **the darkness shall cover the earth and gross darkness the people**; *but the LORD shall arise upon thee, and His glory shall be seen upon thee. And the Gentiles shall come to thy light, and kings to the brightness of thy rising.*

Isaiah 60:1-3

This is news of great joy! God was to change the government over all the Earth. **The coming of the Messiah would neither be a partial victory nor one of phases. It was to be radical! Culminating! Extremely Powerful! It would crush the head of the devil forever! It would snatch the keys of death and hell and it would seat Jesus as King of kings over the whole Earth forever.**

The Father will stop dwelling in a Temple of stone and will make His tabernacle in the hearts of those who believed in Him.

Jesus came in the flesh to overcome death, sin and sickness and to change the era of deep darkness into an era of light. He came to substitute that which was only a type and shadow for what is True. He came to bring a New Covenant, a New Government that would change the Heavens and the Earth completely.

The Spirit of Christ prophesied two great Eras, which even the heathen acknowledge: *Before Christ* and *After Christ*.

Allow me to elaborate further on this concept. We are looking at a clear division between two great Eras:

- One of darkness and one of Redemption.

- An Old Covenant and a New Covenant.

- The earthly things that were a shadow of what was to come, and the heavenly ones that are His Kingdom on Earth.

- The Heavens separated from man and the Heavens united with man.

- The old creature and the new creature.

- Old things passed away and all things are made New.

- The earthly *Jerusalem* in the Old Covenant, the *Jerusalem* above in the New Covenant.

- The old wine skins and the new wineskins (God's people in the Old Testament and God's people in the New).

- The old wine and the new wine.

- The former Levitical Priesthood and the new Priesthood according to the Order of Melchizedek.

If we do not understand the first and grandiose First Coming of the Messiah and the power it brings, that He already sat on His throne, we will continue to wait for Him to come and do what He has already done, which is a wrong perception of the second coming.

I will go into detail about the work of the Messiah in chapter 7, and therefore many issues still surrounded in much confusion shall become clear to us.

Dr. Ana Méndez Ferrell

Before going into a full interpretation of the ***Book of Revelation***, I feel it's important to itemize and understand previously mentioned principles in the Heart of God, which are key to understanding it.

SECTION 2

THE FUNDAMENTAL THEMES IN THE BOOK OF REVELATION

APOCALYPSE The Revelation of Jesus Christ

The central theme in the ***Book of Revelation*** is "**The Revelation of Jesus Christ as Sovereign King of the Universe**". Shortly before the great judgment over *Jerusalem* in the year Seventy and before the *Roman Empire* was destroyed, Jesus appears to John in ALL His glory,

The new century was about to begin: the Age of Light and of the Manifestation of Christ in the heart of the believers. Before His ascension, Jesus spent 40 days teaching the disciples about The Kingdom of God. He was about to go up to Heaven and take the throne of Majesty on High and wanted to make it was very clear for them to understand what was about to happen after His departure. His Kingdom was to be established in the midst of men when the Holy Spirit descended upon all flesh. God is One and He would come to occupy Earth once again.

God left them basic principles on what He was about to do on Earth; if we understand them, they will steer us into revelation. The comprehension of biblical prophecy is not an issue of understanding or a play on words but instead in understanding the global principle in God's thinking. On the other hand, we must also consider the *Time* when it was written in and *For Whom* it was spoken to. And even thought the whole Scripture is alive and a spiritual tool for the Church, it was written and addressed primarily to the people of Israel. Trying to understand Biblical prophecy, while ignoring the historical context that Israel lived in the first century, inevitably would lead us to wrong conclusions. ***(In Instrument # 2 at the end of this book we make a resume of the history of those days.)***

Jesus left us these fundamental principles and we need to understand to interpret the prophecy in the ***Book of Revelation***:

- New Heaven and New Earth
- The Work of the Messiah in His First Coming
- God's Tabernacle with Men
- The New *Jerusalem*
- The Wedding Feast of the Lamb
- The Destruction of *Babylon*
- The Reigning of Christ
- The Abode of God in the Clouds
- The Supreme Court of God's Judgments

Following these primary themes, we encounter secondary themes derived from the first ones that give us the details how Heaven and Earth operate in harmony. Amongst these are: the heavenly battles, the tribulations, the organization of the kingdom of darkness against the Light and the operation of the diverse angels.

6   A NEW HEAVEN AND A NEW EARTH

In the previous chapter, we established the division of the two major *Periods* or *Eras* that shape Biblical history in the Old Testament and the Messianic Era. This understanding serves as a guideline to interpret what Scripture refers to when it talks about "new Heavens" and "new Earth".

> *And I saw a new Heaven and a new Earth, for the first heaven and the new earth had passed away.*
>
> Revelation 21:1a

1. Does God Want To Destroy The Earth?

God loves the Earth, which He filled with His Glory through His Son and does not want to destroy it. He entered into covenant with Noah and that covenant remains forever.

> *And I will remember My covenant which is between Me and you and every living creature of all flesh, and the waters shall no more become a flood to destroy all flesh. And the rainbow shall be in the cloud; and I will look upon it, that I may remember the everlasting covenant between God and every living creature of all flesh that is upon the earth.*
>
> Genesis 9:15-16

God would not enter into an eternal covenant with man and Creation not to destroy them by water and then destroy everything by fire. It would be like ironically saying: *"I enter into a covenant with you not to kill you by the sword but I will now kill you with a gun."* God does not act in that fashion ever.

God will judge those who destroy the Earth because He loves it and does not want to see it destroyed.

> *" ... And the nations were angry; and Thy wrath is come, and the time of the dead, that they should be judged, and that Thou shouldest give reward unto Thy servants the prophets, and to the saints and them that fear Thy name, small and great,* **and shouldest destroy them that destroy the earth."**
>
> Revelation 11:18

> *One generation passeth away, and another generation cometh; but* **the earth abideth forever.**
>
> Ecclesiastes 1:4

> *And He built His sanctuary like high palaces, like the Earth which* **He hath established forever.**
>
> Psalm 78:69

> *Thy people also shall be all righteous;* **they shall inherit the land forever,** *the branch of My planting, the work of My hands, that I may be glorified.*
>
> Isaiah 60:21

2. The Burning Elements

The conflict arises when people read Chapter 3 in Peter's Second Epistle where it seems to be talking about the Earth burning up in flames. This is but a bad translation into our languages. The Bible needs to be coherent in itself. Initially, this passage talks about the destruction of the wicked.

Fire in Scripture means *"judgment"*. When Scripture talks about a *fire baptism* or that *we shall be tried by fire*, it doesn't mean we will literally burn away. Fire is a purifying instrument. God wants to cleanse the Earth and purify it by judging the ungodly people.

> *But the Day of the Lord will come as a thief in the night, in which the **heavens** shall pass away with a great noise, and the **elements** shall melt with fervent heat.*
>
> *The earth also and the works that are therein shall be burned up. Seeing then that all these things shall be dissolved, what manner of persons ought ye to be in all holy manner of living and godliness, looking for and hastening unto the coming of the Day of God, wherein the **heavens**, being on fire, shall be dissolved and the **elements** shall melt with fervent heat? Nevertheless we, according to His promise, look for new heavens and a new earth, **wherein dwelleth righteousness**.*
>
> *2 Peter 3: 10-13*

We have some key words in this portion that help us interpret it correctly. The first one is *"heavens."* This is the Greek word ***ouranos*[11]**, which means *"an elevated place."* This is referring to the high places, to the *second heaven*, the place from where the powers of darkness reign and induce man to ungodliness and not to the destruction of the Universe. This is cleared up with the second word I highlighted: "elements." In Greek it is ***stoicheion*[12]**, which means *"structure, foundation, rudiment."* This is where the word in English *stoic* is derived from which means: *"affirmed with utmost assurance."*

Now this word does not refer to the physical elements of the universal matter, but to the structures of this world that have ruled over the Earth and that Jesus came to topple. Apostle Peter concludes afterwards that upon destroying these world structures we will enjoy a new Heaven and a new Earth where Righteousness dwells. We do not have to wait for the supposed *"End of the world"* for the Righteousness of God to reign on Earth. His Kingdom is Righteousness, Peace and Joy in the Holy Ghost, and it's already in our midst.

This whole passage acquires greater clarity as we continue reading:

> *And account that the longsuffering of our Lord is salvation, even as our beloved brother* **Paul also, according to the wisdom given unto him, hath written unto you, as also in all his epistles, speaking in them of these things.**

---

[11] *3772., oo-ran-os´; perhaps from the same as 3735 (through the idea of elevation); the sky; by extension, heaven (as the abode of God); by implication, happiness, power, eternity; specially, the Gospel (Christianity): — air, heaven(-ly), sky.*

[12] *4747 . stoicheion stoy-khi´-on; neuter of a presumed derivative of the base of 4748; something orderly in arrangement, i.e. (by implication) a serial (basal, fundamental, initial) constituent (literally), proposition (figuratively): — element, principle, rudiment.*

Dr. Ana Méndez Ferrell

> ***Therein are some things hard to understand****, which those who are unlearned and unstable wrest, as they do also the other Scriptures, unto their own destruction.*
>
> *2 Peter 3:15-16*

We see Peter here quoting Apostle Paul who talks about these things in almost all of his epistles. This is exceedingly key since NOWHERE in his epistles does Paul talk about the Earth burning up and being destroyed. However, he does talk about the removing of those things that can be shaken in almost all of them. (*Book of Hebrews*, if Paul is in effect the author.)

> *And these words, "yet once more," signifieth the removing of those things which can be shaken, such as things that are made, that those things which cannot be shaken may remain.*
>
> *Hebrews 12:27*

He writes about the structures of darkness that must be vanquished by the believer who must subject them through Jesus' Victory and put them under his/her feet.

He tells us about how these structures have already been sentenced and everything in Heaven and Earth has been made **new**.

> *Therefore if any man be in Christ, he is a new creature: old things are passed away; behold, **all things** have become new.*
>
> *2 Corinthians 5:17*

Peter exhorted the believers to live in a holy manner because all the structures of wickedness were to be judged in his time and along with them, those who partake of them. Further on I will talk about prophetic times and we will analyze the part that talks about how *a day is like a thousand years* and *a thousand years like a day*. For the time being I am focusing on the meaning of a *new Heaven* and a *new Earth*.

In Peter's passage we just analyzed and saw that Righteousness dwells in this New Heaven and New Earth. Let's look at the analogous passages from the Old Testament, which enlightens us as to its interpretation. Peter was not talking about anything new, he was quoting the scripture in Isaiah 65 where Jehovah had already prophesied these things.

All prophecy in the the Gospels and in the New Testament corresponds to the Old Testament.

3. Isaiah's Prophecy

Let's remember how Jesus opened His disciples' understanding so they could understand how **EVERYTHING in the Law of Moses, in the Psalms and in the Prophets, that had been prophesied about Him, had already been fulfilled.**

> *For, behold, I create new heavens and a new earth; and* ***the former shall not be remembered, nor come into mind****. But be ye glad and rejoice for ever in that which I create; for behold, I create Jerusalem a rejoicing, and her people a joy. And I will rejoice in Jerusalem, and joy in My people; and the voice of weeping shall be no more heard in her, nor the voice of crying.*

Dr. Ana Méndez Ferrell

There shall be no more thence an infant of days, nor an old man that hath not filled his days; for the child shall die a hundred years old; but the sinner being a hundred years old shall be accursed. And they shall build houses and inhabit them; and they shall plant vineyards and eat the fruit of them. They shall not build and another inhabit; they shall not plant and another eat; for as the days of a tree are the days of My people, and Mine elect shall long enjoy the work of their hands.

They shall not labor in vain, **nor bring forth for trouble**; *for they are the seed of the blessed of the LORD, and their offspring with them. And it shall come to pass, that before they call, I will answer; and while they are yet speaking, I will hear. The wolf and the lamb shall feed together, and the lion shall eat straw like the bullock; and dust shall be the serpent's meat. They shall not hurt nor destroy in all My holy mountain," saith the LORD."*

Isaiah 65:17-25

When we read this passage with the preconceived idea that the Earth will be destroyed along with the entire Universe, we imagine a new celestial planet. We are unable to conceive this to be true for our days because the Church continues weeping, continues getting sick, many die young and millions are in lack. In the natural we are not seeing the wolf and the lamb feeding together or children that die a hundred years old. We therefore develop a theology according to *what we don't have* and not according to what was already **conquered by Jesus' resurrection and enthronement.**

APOCALYPSE The Revelation of Jesus Christ

The New Testament declares that old things have passed away and all things have been made new. This points again to the two Eras: the Old and the New.

"*I bring joy to Jerusalem and rejoicing to her people*" are promises that have to do with Messiah's first coming. He himself spoke it when He declared to them that the Spirit of the Lord was upon Him to bring the good news, liberty to the captives and joy to those in mourning. *(Luke 4:18)*

The key passage in *Isaiah 65* is: *They shall not labor in vain or **bring forth children for sudden terror or calamity;** for they shall be the descendants of the blessed of the Lord, and their offspring with them.*

If we part from the erroneous idea that this passage refers to a new celestial planet, and not to the Earth as it is now, we find ourselves in a conflict. How come it says here we will no longer bring forth children for calamity? Those who have interpreted this passage in this way also say that in this new Earth the children of God shall have a resurrected body resembling that of the angels, who can no longer bear children. This is based in the words Jesus spoke, saying:

*But they which shall be counted worthy to obtain that world and the resurrection from the dead, neither marry, nor are given in **marriage**:*
Neither can they die any more: for they are equal unto the angels; and are the children of God, being the children of the resurrection.

Luke 20:35-36

This passage therefore has nothing to do with a new planet but with a new Heaven and a new Earth in Jesus; with the Rulership of the King of kings, Who now governs the Earth.

On one end, when Jesus makes us "new creatures," He doesn't have to physically destroy us. We are made new in our spirit and in our soul. The same thing therefore applies for the Earth to be made "new," it doesn't have to burn up and disappear from the Universe; it's renewed by the Glory of Jesus who fills it all in all.

4.1. There Will Be No More Weeping

Now, why does it say there will be no more weeping? This refers to the ensuing terrible pain when people died in the time before the coming of the Messiah. Death had not been vanquished and the idea of dying was dreadful. When a loved one died, it was devastating to think they had gone to a gloomy, cold and abysmal place. The idea per se was unbearable to the heart of men, but Jesus came and defeated death. Today, those of us who belong to Him, even though we undergo a necessary period of mourning for our soul to adjust to the loss, we rejoice that our loved ones are in Heaven with the Lord if they were saved. God is not a God of the dead but of the living and our beloved who departed in Christ are alive and not dead.

Jesus had the fullness of the Deity in Him. He was One with the Father. He was The Kingdom of God walking among the living and regardless; He wept when Lazarus died and when He predicted the destruction of *Jerusalem*.

In The Kingdom of God, in The New Earth and in The New Heaven He gave us, every tear is wiped away.

4.2. For The Child Shall Die A Hundred Years Old

Why then, did Isaiah say: *"for the child shall die a hundred years old"*? This speaks about longevity and the power of resurrection that indwells the true believer, who has been born of the Spirit.

> *And so it is written, "The first man Adam became a living being. The last Adam became a life-giving spirit."*
>
> 1 Corinthians 15:45

In like manner, when death reigns in those who do not have Christ, it progresses until it deteriorates their bodies and takes them away; resurrection reigns over those who believe, quickening and rejuvenating their mortal body.

4.3. The Wolf And The Lamb

> *"The wolf and the lamb shall feed together, and the lion shall eat straw like the bullock; and dust shall be the serpent's meat. They shall not hurt nor destroy in all My holy mountain," saith the LORD."*
>
> Isaiah 65:25

This is a type of the Church and the different personalities in people who draw near to The Kingdom of God.

We call Jesus *a lamb* and also *a lion*. He said He would send us out as sheep among wolves. These wolves refers to those who were evil people, convert, then come to the Kingdom and dwell together with us.

Zephaniah talks to us about this same zoo morphology.

> *Her princes in her midst are roaring lions; Her judges are evening wolves, that leave not a bone till morning*
>
> *Zephaniah 3:3*

If we open our hearts, we will be able to grasp for ourselves these truths God already bestowed upon us. But if we see them as a reality for a new planet, we shall never possess the fullness of what Jesus did for us.

> *... and hath raised us up together and made us sit together in heavenly places in Christ Jesus,*
>
> *Ephesians 2:6*

7 THE WORK OF MESSIAH IN HIS FIRST COMING

1. The devil stole The Glory and The Essence of The First Coming from us

This is our second basic theme of interpretation needful to understand the truths of the ***Book of Revelation.***

> *And I heard a loud voice saying in Heaven, "Now have come salvation and strength, and the Kingdom of our God, and the power of His Christ; for the accuser of our brethren is cast down, who accused them before our God day and night."*
>
> ***Revelation 12:10***

Part of the problem we find ourselves in, is that in many of the cases there is no clarity as to what was the objective of Christ's First Coming.

Most Christians are waiting with great expectation the Second Coming of Christ hoping it will be sooner rather than later. Meanwhile God is calling out from Heaven:

"I need you to understand My First Coming to begin with!"

We have been satisfied with only one fragment of His work: that He came to save us from sin so He can eventually take us to Heaven.

The majority of Christians are stagnated in that truth and haven't been taught the Fullness and what the Magnificent Messiah came to do on Earth. The result is that they're living in terrible defeat with problems they have no business living in. And furthermore, believing that the good things they are waiting for to happen for them will only happen when Jesus returns for them. As long as we continue to see everything in the far-off future we will never feel challenged to possess today all the Blessings, the Power and the Authority Jesus bought for us.

We can only receive from God that which we believe He has granted us. It then becomes important to understand what He did, so a misinterpretation of the Word does not rob us of our inheritance.

To belong to Jesus implies being a people different from the rest of the world, not only in our ideology of salvation but also in the Powerful Manifestation of Who Jesus is in us.

Jesus came to manifest His Father and this is our mission too. As true sons and daughters of God, we are here to manifest the Father in all His Power and Sovereignty. We will only have the faculty to beget sons and daughters of God according to the measure we reveal the Father through our own lives.

Handing out salvation tracts is lovely but it doesn't manifest the Life of the Father, nor does it reproduce sons and daughters of the Spirit.

The world has to see in us a people who doesn't get sick, who lacks nothing, but instead who gives everything; people brimming with life and vigor, even in their old age; a people who have the most extraordinary solutions to society's problems. A people who know how to use the Power of God to change every circumstance, who know how to appease storms and bring rain during a drought; a people like there has never been time after time, throughout the many generations.

For this to happen, we need to know *"The Gospel of the Kingdom"* and understand its significance in our lives.

2. Jesus Came To Bring The Kingdom Of His Father

Jesus came to establish *a Kingdom*, not to establish *churches*. The Church is the congregation of believers that form part of the King of kings' Governmental System. A kingdom cannot be divided against itself. The 40-thousand+ Christian denominations, which exist today, have no power to change the world; only the unified Kingdom of God can achieve this. If we understand the true and powerful mission of our Messiah, we will be able to unite and transform our nations.

During His manifestation on Earth, Jesus constantly preached about The Kingdom of God as something nearby.

> *... and saying, "The time is fulfilled, and the Kingdom of God is at hand. Repent ye and believe the Gospel."*
>
> *Mark 1:15*

He commanded the preaching of the Gospel of the Kingdom and not the dispensation of Grace.

A P O C A L Y P S E   The Revelation of Jesus Christ

And as ye go, preach, saying, `The Kingdom of Heaven is at hand.'
Heal the sick, cleanse the lepers, raise the dead, cast out devils. Freely ye have received; freely give.

Matthew 10:7-8

It's important to understand that Jesus came to bring the Kingdom of His Father and to prepare that first generation to enter in and govern together with Him. He came to give us spacious entry into the Kingdom not when we die or for an uncertain future, but for the here and now.

The Gospel, which is *the Good News*, only makes sense to the extent that the work of The Cross is effective for us while we are alive. Jesus did not take in His body our sins, our sicknesses and our grief for us to enjoy this only after we die.

The Good News is that The Cross defeated the devil and death so we could live in holiness, in health, in joy, in righteousness and in prosperity while we are alive.

What sense does it make to preach to the poor and to the sick a future Kingdom without a solution to their current problems? Should we call it "*Good News?*"

If the Kingdom is not in our midst, as many suppose, postponing it until the second coming of Christ, then the work of the Cross, and the Good News of the Gospel are senseless.

Why would Jesus send us to preach something that could not be fulfilled until we got to Heaven? Why did He say that "*the latter glory of this house would be greater than the former*" unless this was going to be fulfilled? (The former house is the *Old Covenant;* the latter, the *New.*)

If He came to restore that which had been lost, *"that"* being the dominion God gave Adam to rule over the Earth, why did He said "***It is finished***" if we needed to wait more than 2000 years? Jesus came so everything would return to be as His Father had created it at the beginning: God ruling from Heaven and man in fellowship with Him, ruling on Earth.

He came to unite Heaven and Earth once again reconciling them through The Cross, not sometime in the future but from His death at The Cross.

> *... and having made peace through the blood of His cross, by Him to reconcile all things unto Himself -- by Him, I say, whether they be things on earth or things in heaven.*
>
> *Colossians 1:20*

We can see from the New Testament scripture that is was clear to the apostles how God had returned to us our Fellowship with Him, the Dominion and the Kingdom.

> *Therefore,* **we receiving a Kingdom** *which cannot be moved, let us have grace whereby we may serve God acceptably, with reverence and godly fear*
>
> *Hebrews 12:28*

> *Fear not, little flock, for it is your Father's good pleasure* **to give you the Kingdom***.*
>
> *Luke 12:32*

In this passage Jesus was encouraging them not to fear because He had come to establish the Kingdom, not for when they were already dead but for whenever they felt they had a reason to fear.

Before the outpouring of the Holy Spirit, Jesus taught His apostles about the Kingdom. They needed to know how the Kingdom was going to manifest and how they should reign by the Spirit. Why would He have talked about something that was to manifest in 2,000 plus years during the most important period of His Ministry?

He wasn't talking to them about a "2000 year grace period", as some preach today, He talked to them about *The Kingdom* He had come to establish.

Nowhere in Scripture does Jesus establish a *"dispensation of grace"* between His ascension and the establishment of His Kingdom. This was never foretold in the Old Testament nor did Jesus ever speak about such a thing.

The Old Testament never separates the Messiah from His Kingdom. For all Jews throughout the ages the coming of the Messiah was along with the establishment of God's Kingdom.

It was in the mid XIX century that a man called *John Nelson Darby* came up with the idea of *Dispensacionalism or Sectarian Theology*, making a separation between Israel and the Church and this from the Kingdom.

In this theology that flooded the Evangelical Church, Darby created and era or dispensation in which the Church is not part of the Kingdom. He established that the Kingdom will only come to pass in the future after a *"Great Tribulation."*

Even though his ideas became very popular, they require a serious revision since they were created way before the outpouring of the Holy Spirit in 1906, thus they are filled with errors.

It is very important to analyze why do we believe what we believe, and what are the sources of so many doctrines that we have been dragging around for centuries, passing them from generation to generation. It is time to analize, correct, and truly bring the right foundation to what we believe.

Jesus trained His disciplesto preach the Gospel, to establish The Kingdom of God and to prepare the believers for the great manifestion of His judgement that would come over that generationthat took place in the year 70 A.D.

> *To these also He showed Himself alive after His passion by many infallible proofs, being seen by them forty days, and speaking of the things pertaining to the Kingdom of God.*
> *Acts 1:3*

Jesus said *when seeking The Kingdom of God and His righteousness and all these things would be added unto you.* He then mentions the pertinent matters to our sustenance here on Earth.

> *Therefore take no thought, saying, 'What shall we eat?' or 'What shall we drink?' or 'Wherewith shall we be clothed?' (For after all these things do the Gentiles seek.)*
>
> *For your heavenly Father knoweth that ye have need of all these things.*

But seek ye first the Kingdom of God and His righteousness, and all these things shall be added unto you.

Matthew 6:31-33

What sense does this make to say this, if the Kingdom would only manifest after 2000 years plus?

He told the Pharisees and the Priests *where* and *when* His Kingdom would manifest:

Now when He was asked by the Pharisees when the kingdom of God would come, He answered them and said, "The kingdom of God does not come with observation; nor will they say, "See here!' or 'See there!' For indeed, the kingdom of God is within you."

Luke 17:20-21

If God's will was to establish a Kingdom in a future millennium, Jesus would have said so. Contrary to this He said, "*The Kingdom of God is in your midst.*"

Also, when He referred to John the Baptist as the *greatest* of the Old Testament prophets and as the *greatest* among them that were born of women, but then He pointed him out as the *least* in The Kingdom of God.

Verily I say unto you, among them that are born of women, there hath not risen a greater than John the Baptist; notwithstanding, he that is least in the Kingdom of Heaven is greater than he.

Dr. Ana Méndez Ferrell

> *And from the days of John the Baptist until now, the Kingdom of Heaven suffereth violence, and the violent take it by force.*
>
> *Matthew 11:11-12*

Those born of the Spirit and water are greater than those born of women, even if they were once a great prophet. **The Kingdom is not a place, it is a Person, it is Jesus Himself. To enter His Kingdom is to enter Him, Jesus, and He enters us.** This makes us greater than those who were only anointed but were never born of God.

The Kingdom is for those who take it by force here on Earth. Jesus would not have used this verbiage if He were only referring to those who died and went to Heaven by faith and by grace.

The name of Jesus underwent a Glory-to-Glory transformation. He was born with the name of *Jesus of Nazareth*, originally *Yeshua*. Upon being baptized, the anointing of the Father came upon Him and He became *Jesus the Christ* or *Messiah*, which means "The Anointed of God". But in ascending to the Throne of Glory and seating at the right hand of the Father, He was given a new name, a name that is above all names: **Yeshua, The Lord.**

> *... that at the name of Jesus every knee should bow, of things in Heaven and things on earth and things under the earth,*
> *... and that every tongue should confess that Jesus Christ is Lord, to the glory of God the Father*
>
> *Philippians 2:10-11*

In Timothy's first epistle, Paul refers to Jesus as "King of kings and Lord of lords."

> *... which He in His times shall show -- He who is the blessed and only Potentate, the King of kings and Lord of Lords,*
>
> *1 Timothy 6:15*

Paul does not transfer the Lordship or the Rulership of Jesus Christ to a time in the future, and nobody in the present-day Church has an issue in calling Him in this manner or believing that He is seated at the right hand of the Father in Majesty.

Peter, on the day of Pentecost, acknowledges Him already in His Lordship.

> *"Therefore let all the house of Israel know assuredly that God has made this Jesus, whom you crucified, both Lord and Christ."*
>
> *Acts 2:36*

Now if He is seated at the right hand of the Father and has already been crowned King of Kings, why is it that many don't believe that He reigns? They think He will only reign when He physically sits on the throne in the earthly *Jerusalem* and meanwhile, what is He doing in the Highest at the Father's right hand? Is he scratching His head waiting to reign someday and deliver us from our misery and our problems?

Nowhere in the Gospels did Jesus ever say that He would come back and be seated as a king in Jerusalem. To the contrary, He said that He would NOT be seated in Jerusalem.

Dr. Ana Méndez Ferrell

> *Now when He was asked by the Pharisees when the kingdom of God would come, He answered them and said, "The kingdom of God does not come with observation; nor will they say, "See here!' or 'See there!' For indeed, the kingdom of God is within you."*
>
> Luke 17:20-21

When He said: nor will they say, "See here!' or 'See there!' he was standing in Jerusalem before the Pharisees.

These words produced the irrational wrath that compelled the Pharisees to crucify Jesus, since they were expecting a Messiah that would be a King on Earth. This same way of thinking has greatly contaminated the Church.

This is of vital importance, the apostate Israel of those days wanted the Messiah to sit as an earthly king in Jerusalem. If this was the Father's will, Jesus would have said something like this: "Be not afraid, the time will come when I will come back and reign on the earth." But He never said anything, not even close to that. What He said was the opposite: **"nor will they say, 'See here!' or 'See there!' For indeed, the Kingdom of God is within you."**

Jesus also affirmed:

> *Jesus said to her, "Woman, believe Me, the hour is coming when you will neither on this mountain, nor in Jerusalem, worship the Father.*
>
> John 4:21

If His plan was to come one day and sit in Jerusalem, why did He say this to the Samaritan woman?

The former Jerusalem, the earthly one, is not going to be any more the Head quarters for The Kingdom of God. Jesus came to bring the Kingdom of the Spirit and to establish the Heavenly Jerusalem. That is why in 70 A.D. He destroyed the Temple and the former city.

What sense does it make, to bring down the former Temple, in order to make His new tabernacle within men, and then to rebuild the same temple He destroyed?

If this were true, what would happen to the temple within our spirits? Would we have to renounce to it, to go back into a temple made of stone?

To even think that Jesus would only come to reign in the future is to take away from Him His purpose and His Kingship.

No king is ever been crowned nor does he sit on the throne lest it be to exert his authority.

The truth is, Jesus is King of kings and Lord of lords and He is reigning jointly with all of those who have understood they ARE HIS BODY. If the Head reigns, the body reigns jointly with it.

Salvation consists in acknowledging that He reigns as Sovereign Lord.

> *... that if thou shalt confess with thy mouth the Lord Jesus, and shalt believe in thine heart that God hath raised Him from the dead, thou shalt be saved.*
>
> *Romans 10:9*

Dr. Ana Méndez Ferrell

He said *"My Kingdom is not of this world."*

His Kingdom is of the Spirit, that is why no one can see the Kingdom except those who are born of water and of the Spirit.

The devil doesn't care if we call Jesus "*Lord*" as long as we don't acknowledge Him in His ruling Authority, seated at the right hand of the Father, ruling our lives and our nations. The truth is, when we see Him in His Kingdom, our infirmities, problems and pains are gone. Therefore since all these things are under His feet, when we are ruling and reigning with Him, they are also under ours.

The *Jerusalem* on Earth, its Temple and its history are but a shadow of the things that were to come when Truth manifested, and this was the Coming of Messiah in the flesh.

> *For if He were on earth, He should not be a priest, seeing that there are priests who offer gifts according to the law, and who serve unto the copy and shadow of heavenly things, as Moses was admonished by God when he was about to make the tabernacle. For," See," saith He, "that thou make all things according to the pattern shown to thee on the mount."*
>
> *But now hath He obtained a more excellent ministry, by how much also He is the Mediator of a better covenant, which was established upon better promises.*
>
> *Hebrews 8:4-6*

The *Heavenly Jerusalem* reigns today made up of converted Jews and Gentiles. God made ONE nation out of the two.

> *"But he who was of the bondwoman was born according to the flesh, but he of the freewoman was by promise." These things are an allegory, for these are the two covenants: The one is from Mount Sinai, which engenders bondage; this is Hagar.*
>
> *For this Hagar is Mount Sinai in Arabia and answereth to Jerusalem as it is now, and is in bondage with her children.*
>
> *But the Jerusalem, which is above, is free, and is the mother of us all.*
>
> *...*
>
> *Now we, brethren, as Isaac was, are the children of promise*
>
> Galatians 4:23-26 and 28

Today many people and churches who are not living in the Power of the Kingdom purchased for us at the price of The Cross await the Second Coming for Jesus to bring them the Kingdom and heal their sickness and wipe away every tear. Dear reader, He already did this during His First Coming and it will become clearer further on when we get to the understanding of the **New Jerusalem.**

The Second Coming is not related to being redeemed from the devil and his works. That is part of The First Coming.

I have Jewsh blood in me, and I pray for the salvation of Israel, as I do for the rest of the world. But my aim is not for the earthly Jerusalem as my final quest, but the heavenly one for we are under the covenant of The Spirit and not under that of the flesh.

The Kingdom of God is Heavenly, not worldly, Jesus reigns seated at the Right Hand of the Father from the *Jerusalem* above.

Dr. Ana Méndez Ferrell

IF THEN you have been raised with Christ [to a new life, thus sharing His resurrection from the dead], aim at and seek the [rich, eternal treasures] that are above, where Christ is, seated at the right hand of God (which means ruling and reigning.)

Colossians 3:1 *Amplified*
(Capital letters added by the author)

And set your minds and keep them set on what is above (the higher things), **not on the things that are on the earth.**
For [as far as this world is concerned] you have died, and your [new, real] life is hidden with Christ in God.

Colossians 3:2-3 Amplified

Now we, brethren, as Isaac was, are children of promise.
But, as he who was born according to the flesh then persecuted him who was born according to the Spirit, even so it is now.
Nevertheless what does the Scripture say? "Cast out the bondwoman and her son, for the son of the bondwoman shall not be heir with the son of the freewoman." So then, brethren, we are not children of the bondwoman but of the free.

Galatians 4:28-31

I want to make it clear that if Jesus is not reigning in His Kingdom, and if He is not yet seated on His Throne of Glory, then He has NOT been crowned as King of kings either, and this stance creates a gigantic conflict.

This stance leaves us in a limbo of uncertainty where nothing is happening between Christ's ascension and His coming in the clouds. Thinking that Jesus is not yet ruling in His Kingdom keeps people in a state of passivity and waiting, just holding on till He comes back.

At this moment in time, the Church in general lacks authority. On one hand we say "we are kings and priests" yet on the other hand, deep inside we consider it solely as a theological position but not as a reality.

The majority of God's people do not know how to rule, how to take authority or how to change their circumstances because the Kingdom has been transferred to an uncertain future. To those who think this way, the Kingdom is only a hope but not a reality and this is the reason the devil is winning most battles in their lives.

If this state of limbo or waiting period is right, then the glorious Gospel of Jesus Christ is senseless in our lives. We live in the same pain, lack and infirmity as any non-convert and the only thing we possess is our hope for when we die or when Christ returns.

If this is true, all the promises we previously read regarding the Kingdom make no sense either.

As I stated previously at the beginning of this chapter, we are living in perilous times where our preconceived ideas box us in and distort us so we are unable to see the Glory of our Messiah, as it was during the First Coming.

> *But if our Gospel be hid, it is hid to those who are lost, whose unbelieving minds the god of this world hath blinded, lest the light of the glorious Gospel of Christ, who is the image of God, should shine unto them.*
>
> *2 Corinthians 4:3-4*

Nowadays a Gospel of Grace and Salvation is preached but the Light of the Gospel of the Glory of Christ, the Lord of lords reigning in full Power and Authority continues to be veiled for those who live in disbelief; especially disbelief about the already present Kingdom and its Power.

People are so "step-by-step"-structured as to what has to happen, before, during, and after the Coming of Jesus that the same thing that happened to the Scribes and the Doctors of the Law could happen to them. If Jesus does not move according to their theologies and preconceived ideas, they will not see Him.

At this moment in time, there are hundreds of thousands of us living and experiencing the Power and the Majesty of The Kingdom of God. The Kingdom is not a far-away hope but instead, it is a visible, palpable and demonstrative reality.

The First Coming of Messiah is ABSOLUTELY POWERFUL and we have to understand and value everything that was PAID for us at The Cross of Calvary to give us access to the New Life in The Kingdom of God.

I invite you to be brave and de-structure yourself to find that neutral and humble position so the Heavens may open further over your life and His Holy Spirit will announce what He is saying to you.

I understand that I am writing things here that are strong and hard to receive. This may create a clash inside of many, due to the erroneous structures we have formed within.

Sometimes it is necesassary to stop reading and pray, but I encourage you to finish reading this book. Several things will become more clear as you keep reading, and it will change your life.

The Church needs to rethink why she believes what she believes.She needs to search for the Truth through the Spirit of Revelation that is Jesus Christ and cast away a lot of fables and wrong theologies that have been passed on from former generations without even asking where they come from or if they are coherent with the Spirit of Christ and with God's plan.

8. GOD'S TABERNACLE WITH MAN AND THE NEW *JERUSALEM*

1. A Tabernacle Of Flesh

We have already analyzed our first and second theme: *New Heavens and New Earth* and *The Works of the Messiah*. Now we will touch on the third theme: *God's Tabernacle with men*. It's important to analyze them and be able to understand the different themes in the **Book of Revelation** to develop a suitable eschatology. If this theme is made clear to us, many of the confusing jigsaw puzzle pieces will fall into place.

History has established that the physical temple in *Jerusalem* was destroyed in the year 70 AD. Through His death and resurrection, Jesus was to establish a new tabernacle inside the believers: the Temple of God in the Spirit, which was to replace the one, made of stone.

> *Jesus answered and said unto them, "Destroy this temple, and in three days I will raise it up."*
> *John 2:19*

> *What? Know ye not that your body is the temple of the Holy Ghost which is in you and which ye have from God, and that ye are not your own.*
> *1 Corinthians 6:19*

> *Now therefore, ye are strangers and foreigners no more, but **fellow citizens** with the saints, and of the household of God. Ye are built upon the foundation of the apostles and prophets, Jesus Christ Himself being the chief cornerstone, in whom all the building, fitly framed together, groweth unto a **holy temple** in the Lord, in Whom ye also are built together for a habitation of God **through the Spirit.***
>
> *Ephesians 2:19-22*

These passages of Scripture are the fulfillment of the words spoken by the prophet Ezekiel:

> *Moreover I will make a covenant of peace with them. It shall be an **everlasting covenant** with them. And I will place them, and multiply them, and will set My sanctuary in the midst of them for evermore. **My tabernacle also shall be with them. Yea, I will be their God, and they shall be My people**. And the heathen shall know that I, the LORD, do sanctify Israel, when My sanctuary shall be in the midst of them for evermore.*
>
> *Ezekiel 37:26-27*

All theologies agree that this prophecy is fulfilled with Christ's First Coming when the Lord makes His abode in us, His children.

> *Jesus answered and said unto him, "If a man loves Me, he will keep My words; and My Father will love him, and We will come unto him and **make Our abode with him.**"*
>
> *John 14:23*

The Holy Spirit living in us makes it possible for the Father and the Son to make their abode in our spirit, which God transforms into the new ark where He establishes His Presence.

These theologies are all in agreement that this is not for the future but for us today. However, when we read this same scripture in the ***Book of Revelation***, we no longer believe this is for today but for the future. It's in this confusion where the devil steals from us the power to reign with Christ.

> *And I, John, saw the holy city, New Jerusalem, coming down from God out of Heaven, prepared as a bride adorned for her husband. And I heard a great voice out of Heaven, saying, "Behold, the tabernacle of God is with men, and He will dwell with them; and they shall be His people, and God Himself shall be with them and be their God.*
>
> *Revelation 21:2-3*

This confusion occurs because we have deeply rooted theologies in our minds as to how Revelation 21 HAS TO HAPPEN after the destruction of the Earth, so we are unable to see how this passage of Scripture is exactly the same one Ezekiel's prophesied regarding Christ's first coming. The ***Book of Revelation*** is not an isolated revelation, it is coherent with the Old Testament which confirms it.

God is not going to establish His Tabernacle in the midst of men in the future, He already did it. The Church is His Temple, He legitimately abides in the believers. To think that He has not made His Tabernacle in us is to deny the very heart of the Gospel.

Therefore, if this is a fundamental truth, it will guide me to correctly interpret the rest of Chapter 21. The second concept, which gives me the absolute certainty that this passage refers to something that already happened is:

And He said unto me, "It is done! I am Alpha and Omega, the beginning and the end. I will give unto him that is thirsty of the fountain of the Water of Life freely."
Revelation 21:6

These are the same words Jesus uttered before dying. When He said: "***It is finished.***" He clearly made it known that His redemptive work was done; that the Ancient Covenant culminated at that moment, giving way to the New.

We need to understand that when Jesus spoke those words from The Cross, He did not yet live in the heart of any believer. The right to live within us had been lawfully purchased, but it was not manifested until the Day of Pentecost.

Additionally, in this scripture from the **Book of Revelation**, Jesus calls us to drink from the fountain of life, which is clearlya call to salvation, this is what He told the Samaritan woman at the well. He was speaking to a people living in a very dry land under the rulership of death and who needed to drink of Jesus.

This obviously doesn't make sense if Revelation 21 refers to a time in which the Earth has already been supposedly destroyed as it is taught in traditional theology. For them the saved are already in Heaven and the lost are in hell. My question to them is, "Why are there people thirsty in the 'New Earth' if Heaven is not a desert and all of those who are there, are saved."

Let us remember that the *Book of Revelation* was neither written in a chronological order, nor those who compiled it in the fourth century knew the right order in which John received it.

I quickly understood how this drinking from the waters of life refers to a message needed to be conveyed to bring hope to people who still remain under the yoke of sin and of death.

Keeping these principles in mind, while analyzing the rest of Chapter 21.

2. Chapter 21 of The Book Of Revelation

This is one of the most important chapters for our time and it's a true legacy God left for us. The themes we are analyzing, *The Tabernacle of God with men* and *The New Jerusalem* are vital to our walk with Christ and to understand the structure and the function of the Church in our days. Both are found in this passage, therefore understanding it will clear up much of what is confusing.

The chapter begins with the declaration that "*all things have been made new*" From the moment He sits on His Throne at the right Hand of the Father after His ascension, is then the beginning of the Age of the Messiah. Jesus has redeemed Heaven and Earth and an *Age of Light* has now begun.

> *And I saw a new heaven and a new earth, for the first heaven and the first earth had passed away, and there was no more sea.*
> *Revelation 21:1*

The "*sea*" in this Scripture is not referring to the beautiful ocean God created, but to one of three most important regions of death.

The ***Book of Revelation*** talks about three different types of seas:

a. The Sea of God

> *And I saw, as it were, a sea of glass mingled with fire, and them that had gotten the victory over the beast, and over his image, and over his mark, and over the number of his name, standing on the sea of glass and having the harps of God.*
>
> *Revelation 15:2*

b. The Earthly seas, which are the oceans.

c. The Sea, which is a region of death found under the ocean.

> *And the **sea** gave up the dead which were in it; and death and hell delivered up the dead which were in them; and they were judged every man according to their works.*
> *Revelation 20:13*

Note how *"the sea"* gives up its dead here. If these were the oceans and it's alluding to those who drowned in it, then the passage would say: *'The sea gave up its dead and the land its deceased.'* But it doesn't say that. It talks about three spiritual regions from where death rules: the Sea, (also called the abyss), Death, and Hades.

This place of death is also the one that sustains *Babylon*, the great harlot. The angel who decrees its judgment casts a millstone into the region of death, which sustains this spiritual structure. This region is over many peoples and nations.

> *Then a mighty angel took up a stone like a great millstone, and cast it into the **sea**, saying, "Thus with violence shall that great city Babylon be thrown down, and shall be found no more at all.*
> *Revelation 18:21*

> *And I stood upon the sand of the **sea**. And I saw a beast rise up out of the **sea**, having seven heads and ten horns, and upon his horns ten crowns, and upon his heads the name of blasphemy.*
> *Revelation 13:1*

The beast mentioned in **Book of Revelation 13** arises from this region of death. This region of death keeps many nations captive and annihilates people's spiritual lives.

> *And he saith unto me, "The waters which thou sawest, where the whore sitteth, are peoples and multitudes, and nations and tongues.*
> *Revelation 17:15*

3. The New Jerusalem

Beginning on verse 2 of Chapter 21 we see another topic surfacing which is clearly tied to *God's Tabernacle with man* that is the *New Jerusalem*. This is also our *Third Principle of Interpretation*.

Throughout the Pauline epistles we see how the topic of the Heavenly *Jerusalem* is one of the names God uses to refer to His Church. The physical *Jerusalem* was the place where God abided during the Old Covenant. And the *Jerusalem* from above, the Heavenly One, are "*us*" the believers and Jews as well as Gentiles.

> *For this Hagar is Mount Sinai in Arabia and answereth to **Jerusalem** as it is now, and is in bondage with her children. But the **Jerusalem** which is above is free, and is the mother of us all.*
>
> *Galatians 4:25-26*

> *But ye have come unto Mount Zion and unto the city of the living God, the **heavenly** Jerusalem, and to an innumerable company of angels,*
>
> *Hebrews 12:22*

We clearly see how in these two passages the Church born of the Spirit, is the *Heavenly Jerusalem*, and we are the Temple of God, the Heavenly City.

Jesus has already established the Heavenly City in our midst, and He already is The Tree of Life giving life to His body as the vine does to the branches.

The Heavenly City is our design as a glorious Church. The City is God's Tabernacle with man. If the city were for the future then in actuality, we are not God's Temple either.

Do you realize how important it is to understand this topic?

> *And I, John, saw the holy city, New Jerusalem, coming down from God out of Heaven, prepared as a bride adorned for her husband.*
>
> *Revelation 21:2*

Dr. Ana Méndez Ferrell

> *And I heard a great voice out of Heaven, saying, "Behold, **the tabernacle of God is with men**, and He will dwell with them; and they shall be His people, and God Himself shall be with them and be their God.*
>
> Revelation 21:3

As of this moment John was quoting Isaiah Chapter 60. Remember what Jesus said about the fulfillment of these prophecies: that everything concerning Him in the Torah, the Prophets and the Psalms had already been fulfilled. *(Luke 24:44)*

Comparison between Revelation 21 and Isaiah 60

> *And God shall wipe away all tears from their eyes; and there shall be no more death, neither sorrow, nor crying, neither shall there **be any more pain**: for the former things are passed away.*
>
> Revelation 21:4

Parallel to **Isaiah 60:18 and 20b**

> *Violence shall no more be heard in thy land, wasting nor destruction within thy borders; but thou shalt call thy walls Salvation and thy gates Praise.*
>
> *...*
>
> *Thy sun shall no more go down; neither shall thy moon withdraw itself: for the LORD shall be thine everlasting light, and the days of **thy mourning shall be ended**.*

APOCALYPSE The Revelation of Jesus Christ

The sun shall be no more thy light by day, neither for brightness shall the moon give light unto thee; but the LORD shall be unto thee an everlasting light, and thy God thy glory.
Isaiah 60:18 and 20b

And the city had no need of the sun, neither of the moon, to shine in it: for the glory of God did lighten it, and **the Lamb is the light thereof.**
Revelation 21:23

Parallel to **Isaiah 60:19-20a**

The sun shall be no more thy light by day; neither for brightness shall the moon give light unto thee: **but the LORD shall be unto thee an everlasting light,** *and thy God thy glory.*
Thy sun shall no more go down; neither shall thy moon withdraw itself: for the LORD shall be thine everlasting light …
Isaiah 60:19-20a

And the nations of them which are saved shall walk in the light of it: and the kings of the earth do bring their glory and honor into it.
And **the gates of it shall not be shut at all by day***: for there shall be no night there. And they shall bring the glory and honor of the nations into it.*
Revelation 21:24-26

Dr. Ana Méndez Ferrell

Parallel to **Isaiah 60:11**

> *Therefore thy gates shall be open continually;* ***they shall not be shut day nor night;*** *that men may bring unto thee the forces of the Gentiles, and that their kings may be brought.*
> *Isaiah 60:11*

To those who don't live the reality of the invisible Kingdom of the Spirit, these prophecies are incomprehensible. But to those who have united to Jesus in one Spirit, to be the spouse of the Lamb, this is daily living. This same passage in Isaiah begins with the announcement of the work of the Messiah which all of us acknowledge is for our day.

> *Arise, shine, for **thy light is come, and the glory of the LORD is risen upon thee**.*
> *For behold, the darkness shall cover the earth and gross darkness the people; but the LORD shall arise upon thee, and His glory shall be seen upon thee.*
> *And the Gentiles shall come to thy light, and kings to the brightness of thy rising.*
> *Isaiah 60:1-3*

This is the same light that shines full of glory in the Heavenly City who is the Church. He is our only Light that illuminates our understanding.

In the Old Covenant, the land was full of thick dark clouds and deep darkness covered the nations, but when the Messiah overcame He bequeathed to us His Light to illuminate the whole world with it.

APOCALYPSE The Revelation of Jesus Christ

Isaiah, as well as the **Book of Revelation**, talks about the glorious Church, not as one in the future but in the here and now, a Church in the Spirit that believes in God.

It's the Church who has those gates continually open for all who want to freely drink of the *waters of life*. But this is the Church seen from the Heavens, the Church that has entered to possess the Kingdom. These are not those who attend a Christian Church and say "*Lord, Lord.*" Everybody may come in to our Churches and listen to the Word but not everybody can enter the Kingdom, only those who wash their clothes with the Blood of the Lamb, depart from sin and iniquity and take the Kingdom truths by force.

> *But the fearful, and unbelieving, and the abominable, and murderers, and whoremongers, and sorcerers, and idolaters, and all liars, shall have their part in the lake which burneth with fire and brimstone, which is the second death."*
>
> *And there came unto me one of the seven angels, who had the seven vials full of the seven last plagues, and talked with me, saying, "Come hither; I will show thee the bride, the Lamb's wife."*
>
> *And he carried me away in the spirit to a great and high mountain, and showed me that great city, the Holy Jerusalem, descending out of Heaven from God, having the glory of God.*
>
> *And her light was like unto a stone most precious, even like a jasper stone, clear as crystal.*
>
> *Revelation 21:8-11*

These verses are analogous to those we just saw in Isaiah 60. John is talking about God's designs descending from Heaven here. Many people are unable to relate the word "Heaven" to their daily living when they listen to it, because they see it as a place where they will be in the future, alien to their earthly reality.

To Jesus, Heaven and Earth are united in Him. He lived in the Heavens and on Earth at the same time, He moved in both dimensions simultaneously.

> *If I have told you earthly things and ye believe not, how shall ye believe if I tell you of heavenly things? And* ***no man hath ascended up to Heaven, but He that came down from Heaven, even the Son of Man who is in Heaven.***
>
> John 3:12-13

Jesus spoke this long before His ascension to Heaven. He said He went up and came down and that He was in Heaven. The truth is, this is the only authentic way of living in the Kingdom. Jesus opened the way to the Heavens so we could boldly come before His Throne of Grace. Living in the revelation that John lived in, is a commonplace realm to the children of God.

In Jesus, Heaven and Earth have been united; those who are genuinely in Jesus have access to the Heavens just as Jesus had it when He was on Earth.

> *... having made known to us the mystery of His will, according to His good pleasure which He purposed in Himself,*

> *... that in the dispensation of the fullness of the times He might gather together in one all things in Christ,* **both which are in heaven and which are on earth**—*in Him.*
>
> *Ephesians 1:9-10*

Thousands of people are taken up continually to see and experience Heaven's dimensions. If this is still not a reality for you maybe it's because you have never considered the possibility. Dare to believe and take the Kingdom by force for your life!

Religion views Heaven as something up high and far away but Jesus brought it to Earth so we could enjoy it while we are still alive here on Earth.

Jesus prepared the Heavenly City for us so wherever He is, that we may also be.

> *In My Father's house are many mansions; if it were not so, I would have told you. I go to prepare a place for you.*
>
> *And if I go and prepare a place for you, I will come again and receive you unto Myself,* **that where I am, there ye may be also.**
>
> *John 14:2-3*

If Jesus is in us and we are in Him, then our spiritual house is also in our midst.

> *For we know that if our earthly house, this tabernacle, were dissolved, we have a building of God, a house not made with hands, eternal in the heavens.*

> *For in this we groan, earnestly desiring to be clothed about with our house which is from Heaven, that, being so clothed, we shall not be found naked.*
>
> *For we that are in this tabernacle do groan, being burdened, not because we would be unclothed, but clothed about,* ***that mortality might be swallowed up by life.***
>
> 2 Corinthians 5:1-4

We see in this passage how our spiritual house is our true clothing. Paul groans to be clothed with that house. It doesn't come to him by the work of Grace, he has to take it by force through prayer and untold groans. The wonderful result of being clothed in our heavenly clothing is that our mortality is swallowed up by life.

God's Tabernacle is Jesus Himself being formed in us. He is the Kingdom and He is also the city that descends from Heaven.

When I understand this and I pursue it till it becomes a reality in my life, all the mortality of this world cannot touch me.

This is not a manner of speaking or a manner of interpreting Scripture, it's the reality many of us are already living.

The Father as well as the Son manifest in our lives through that heavenly clothing.

> *At that day ye shall know that I am in My Father, and you in Me, and I in you. He that hath My commandments and keepeth them, he it is that loveth Me; and he that loveth*

> *Me shall be loved by My Father, and I will love him and **will manifest Myself to him.***"
>
> *Judas (not Iscariot) said unto Him, **"Lord, how is it that Thou wilt manifest Thyself unto us, and not unto the world?"***
>
> *Jesus answered and said unto him, "If a man love Me, he will keep My words; and My Father will love him, and We will come unto him and **make Our abode with him.***
>
> John 14:20

When God manifests Himself by making His abode with us then we learn how we have been conceived. We no longer see ourselves in our problems and weaknesses but as the powerful sons and daughters of God full of the Glory He already gave us to rule on Earth.

> *If ye then be risen with Christ, seek those things which are above, where Christ sitteth at the right hand of God. Set your affection on things above, not on things on the earth.*
>
> *For ye are dead, and your life is hid with Christ in God. When Christ, who is our life, shall appear, then shall ye also appear with Him in glory.*
>
> Colossians 3:1-4

Let's return to the passage in **Book of Revelation** 21:

> *And the city had no need of the sun, neither of the moon to shine in it; for the glory of God gave it light, and the Lamb is the light thereof.*
>
> Revelation 21:23

Jesus is the Light that illuminates our temple. While on Earth, He took three of His disciples to the top of the mount to show them He Himself was the Kingdom, the Power and the Glory. Moses and Elijah appeared to represent the Law and the Prophets as witnesses to the Glory of God. Jesus shone much more than the noonday sun showing them the Heavenly *Jerusalem* described in the **Book of Revelation**.

The *Heavenly City* is the Body of Jesus composed of living stones who are all the believers in their individual beauty and characteristics. It has the brightness of God on its walls and its make-up is cubed, the same way as the Holy of Holies because the Living God dwells therein. The *Tree of Life* and the *River of Life* are in its center and both are Jesus, who is the Eternal Life and the Water that quickens all who drink of it. It's from within us that the fountain of life springs forth producing the *River of God*.

> *But whosoever drinketh of the water that I shall give him shall never thirst; but the water that I shall give him shall be in him a well of water springing up into everlasting life.*
>
> *John 4:14*

He that has understood what it means to be the Temple of God, knows that his/her spirit are the very altar from where the waters of life flow, and he/she do not allow any contamination to enter. These people don't have to ask God to take them to the Holy of Holies as if it were a place separated from them, they live, breath and feed from it.

Its design is not a pyramid with a man in the summit and the rest underneath but it's a cube representing the united body in harmony, with ONE single head Who is Christ.

Today we have many pyramids as the Church structure, but God has already started a marvelous work in many of them, uniting them by the Spirit to form the true design by which He can rule entire cities and nations. **The design of the Church is a city**, not a whole lot of denominations divided one from another.

Very soon we will see thousands of churches filled with the knowledge of God transforming the pyramidal system into a City-Church and the Glory of God will overflow them.

Its foundation is the apostolic government of Christ, these are apostles and prophets who are not seeking to be seen but instead, they are covered by precious stones, these being their spiritual disciples raised up by pastors, teachers and evangelists to shine forth as the fruit of their true apostleship.

The doors are 12 pearls, because the entrance to the city is entering The Kingdom of God, which is the Pearl of great price. Christ Himself is the Pearl, His Government and His Principles symbolized by the number 12.

The suffering of an oyster makes a pearl when either sand or even a tiny pebble gets inside it. This speaks of Jesus "The Rock" dressed up in Glory by through His sufferings. It is the redemptive work of Jesus at The Cross that gives us access to the Eternal City.

The mission of the City (which is the unity of Christ and His wife) is to shine brightly and carry the Glory of God to the nations. It's the Light that shines over Mount Zion for the illumination of the knowledge of God. She's careful that no uncleanliness enters her and she opens her door to bring in those who are thirsty for the Lord.

She is not divided nor is there competition amongst her own members but she is united at its joints and being built up as a spiritual building.

> *And are built upon the foundation of the apostles and prophets, Jesus Christ himself being the chief corner stone;*
> *In whom all the building fitly framed together groweth unto an holy temple in the Lord: In whom ye also are builded together for an habitation of God through the Spirit.*
> *Ephesians 2:20-22*

The City descends from Heaven because such are the designs of God for His Church who is His Spouse. We marry the Lamb in the dimensions of the Spirit.

9 THE LAMB'S SPOUSE

This is one of the most important subjects the Holy Spirit wants us to understand since it's fundamental to know what has been granted unto us on God's behalf. This is also our fifth theme for interpretation, which will set into place many loose pieces of the "***Book of Revelation*** *jigsaw puzzle*".

Marriage is consummated when a man and woman become one flesh in intimacy, when she becomes flesh of his flesh, bone of his bones; the apostle Paul distinctly writes about this.

> *... for the husband is the head of the wife, even as Christ is the head of the church, and He is the **savior of the body**. Therefore as the church is subject unto Christ, so let the wives be to their own husbands in every thing.*
> *Husbands, love your wives even as Christ also loved the church and gave Himself for it, that He might sanctify and cleanse it with the washing of water by the Word, that He might present it to Himself a glorious church, not having spot or wrinkle or any such thing, but that it should be holy and without blemish. So ought men to love their wives as their own bodies. He hat loveth his wife loveth himself.*

*For no man ever yet hated **his own flesh**, but nourisheth and cherisheth it, even as the Lord the church. For **we are members of His body, of His flesh, and of His bones.** "For this cause shall a man leave his father and mother, and shall be joined unto his wife, and they two shall be one flesh." This is a great mystery, but **I speak concerning Christ and the church.***

Ephesians 5:23-32

But he that is joined unto the Lord is one spirit.

1 Corinthians 6:17

These passages are evidence beyond a doubt that to be the Body of Christ it is necessary to be joined to Him as His wife.

When a man and a woman marry they become one flesh. When we marry Jesus we become ONE SPIRIT with Him. When He said: *"It is finished,"* He meant that the work was done. He completely and absolutely washed us by His blood. There are no more spots or wrinkles in His blood; we are clean as snow. This is the work of **Grace.**

Understanding this makes a complete difference. If I am only Christ's bride waiting to marry Him in the future then I'm still not His Body. The bride has no legal access to anything that belongs to the bridegroom but once married, she has access to everything. Only the wife has the King's checkbook and has open doors for intimacy with Him; the bride has only a hope.

This is a matter of central importance because while we continue waiting for the wedding feast of the Lamb to some uncertain future, we don't have access to anything and this is where the devil robs us of the power, the riches, and our entry into the King's chambers.

Apostle John Eckhardt writes in his book **"Behold I Come Quickly"**:
" The eschatological wedding is connected to the fall of *Babylon*. Both occurred at the end of the age. The whore (covenant breaking and apostate Israel) is judged and a new marriage (new covenant Church) is consummated."

The eschatological wedding is the fulfillment of God's promise to Israel of being betrothed in righteousness (*Hosea 2:19-20*). This betrothal was through Christ and the New Covenant. The New Covenant Church in the first century consisted of both Jews and Gentiles. The invitation to the marriage was given in the first century, and all things were made ready then. *(Matthew 22:1-4)* Some have tried to put the wedding at the end of the Christian age instead of the end of the Jewish age.

The parable of the ten virgins (*Matthew 25*) reflects the betrothal of Christ and His Church. The Lord left to prepare a place for His bride, and would return to take her to the bridal chamber. The five virgins were those prepared for his return, and the five foolish represented those unprepared. Oil represents the anointing and living by the Holy Spirit.

Jesus was speaking to the Jews of His time. The time of betrothal would not last for thousands of years. The betrothal would last for a generation. The marriage of the Lamb would occur shortly *(Revelation 1:1,3; 19:7-9)*. John the Baptist rejoiced because he heard the Bridegroom's voice *(John 3:29)*. This again has a first century application. Jesus the Bridegroom had appeared and began calling His church to the marriage.

The betrothal was prophesied by Hosea *(Hosea 2:19-20)*. Israel's unfaithfulness to the old covenant would result in a new covenant, a new betrothal. The parable of the ten virgins reflects the Jewish wedding custom of Jesus day. The groom would be delayed while he prepared a dwelling for his bride at his father's house. The groom returns for his bride once the dwelling is finished *(John 14:1-3)*. The bride and groom then go in procession to the groom's father's house for the marriage feast."

> *And I heard as it were the voice of a great multitude, and as the voice of many waters, and as the voice of mighty thundering, saying, Alleluia: for the Lord God omnipotent reigneth.*
> *Let us be glad and rejoice, and give honor to him: for the marriage of the Lamb is come, and his wife hath made herself ready.*
> *Revelation 19:6-7*

The reign of God had come and was manifested through the judgments upon *Babylon*. The saints are glad and rejoice because the marriage has arrived and the saints now receive the blessings of the consummated Kingdom. This is what the early church was taught by the apostles to expect and receive in their lifetime.[13]

Jesus prepared the dwelling place, the same way a bridegroom prepares a house for his bride.

> *In my Father's house are many mansions: if it were not so, I would have told you. I go to prepare a place for you.*
>
> *And if I go and prepare a place for you, I will*

---
[13] *"Behold I Come Quickly"* by John Eckhardt, pages 161 and 162

> *come again, and receive you unto myself; that where I am, there ye may be also.*
>
> *John 14:2-3*

Jesus is in the heart of the believers and we are in Him. **This is not for the future, this a Core Truth of The Gospel.**

While studying Chapter 21 of the Book of Revelation, we are clearly seeing that the New Jerusalem is the dwelling place of God among men Here and Now.

Now I want you to notice that the wife of The Lord is indeed the Tabernacle of flesh where He dwells.

> *And I John saw the holy city, new Jerusalem, coming down from God out of heaven, prepared as a bride adorned for her husband.*
> *And I heard a great voice out of heaven saying, Behold, the tabernacle of God is with men, and he will dwell with them, and they shall be his people, and God himself shall be with them, and be their God.*
>
> *Revelation 21: 2-3*

1. The Consummation Of The Marriage Of The Lamb

REVELATION 19

The Church, the Body of Christ is already His wife. What then, is the marriage supper in the ***Book of Revelation***, and how is this wedding manifested in our lives?

APOCALYPSE The Revelation of Jesus Christ

As we have been studying, this is *a Living Book* and *a Kingdom Manual* which qualifies us to rule with Christ. Upon reading Chapter 19 as well as Chapter 21 it becomes clear to us, that this legacy from John is not chronological.

The first thing I want you to notice is that in this much acclaimed passage as *"The wedding supper of the Lamb"* no marriage ceremony is mentioned and the groom is nowhere to be found.

It is important to remember that the titles assigned to the chapters in the Bible are not of divine inspiration. They were put there along with the division of chapters and verse numbers to help the readers of Scripture.

Unfortunately as we read these titles in the **Book of Revelation** they divert us from the true meaning and lock us in according to the mindset of those who drafted them.

Therefore, let us forget the titles and focus in the principles of understanding we are developing.

> *Let us be glad and rejoice and give honor to Him, for the marriage of the Lamb is come, and His wife hath made herself ready."*
>
> *And to her was granted that she should be arrayed in fine linen, clean and white; for the fine linen is the righteousness of saints.*
>
> *And he said unto me, "Write: `Blessed are they **that are called unto the marriage supper of the Lamb.**'" And he said unto me, "These are the true sayings of God."*

Dr. Ana Méndez Ferrell

*And I fell at his feet to worship him. But he said unto me, "See that thou do it not! I am thy fellow servant and one of thy brethren, who hold to the testimony of Jesus. Worship God! For **the testimony of Jesus is the spirit of prophecy."***

Revelation 19:7-10

I emphasized the two key parts to understand what God is attempting to tell us in bold letters. The first thing He wants to show us is the realm in which the union of His Spirit with ours occurs; **this the marriage supper, which is the dimensions of the Spirit where John is receiving the prophecy. Secondly, is how this happens: which is by The Spirit of Prophecy.**

John falls to his feet before the angel because of the impressive visions and revelations he is receiving from God. However the angel clears it up for him to worship God because everything he is seeing and experiencing is the Spirit of Prophecy, which is the Testimony of Jesus.

In other words what the angel of the Lord is saying is: *"Everything you are seeing and experiencing is Jesus Himself, it is the revelation of everything Jesus came to do."* The Spirit of prophecy is the realm where you get to know Him in His fullness because the dimension of the Spirit is Jesus Himself. Jesus and the Heavens are one, and you have to be immersed in Him to experience it.

The blessing is in partaking of the Lord's Supper because when you eat and drink of His Blood, His Spirit and His Life marry you.

To eat and to drink of Him opens our understanding and transfers us to the dimension where He reigns.[14]

---

[14] *You can find the depth of this topic in my book "Eat of my flesh and drink of My Blood."*

The Lord's Supper is to live in Him and to participate in the glory of His judgments over every ungodliness, dining with Him is delighting ourselves in His Righteousness.

> *Do ye not know that the saints shall judge the world? And if the world shall be judged by you, are ye unworthy to judge the smallest matters?*
> *Know ye not that we shall judge angels? How much more, things that pertain to this life?*
>
> *1 Corinthians 6:2-3*

When we dine with Him, is when His Spirit fuses with ours and the Heavens open up for us to understand and to know Christ as **King**, **Ruler** and **Judge of the Universe.**

Jesus unites to that true believer who has left their life of sin to subject themselves to the Lordship of their spouse in Heaven. Many of the church attendees nowadays are still in the engagement stage but they have not married yet. These people have entered into a covenant of salvation and are undergoing a process of regeneration. Jesus considers these as part of Him, but they cannot enjoy the privileges of the wife until their conversion and their surrender to God is a total one. To achieve this, it is necessary to be an overcomer.

> *Behold, I stand at the door and knock. If anyone hears My voice and opens the door, I will come in to him and dine with him, and he with Me. To him who overcomes I will grant to sit with Me on My throne, as I also overcame and sat down with My Father on His throne.*
>
> *Revelation 3:20-21*

To rule means to bring justice to the offended party and judgment to the ungodly; it is also the administration of all of Earth and Heaven's resources.

When our spirit merges with God's in the marriage of the Spirit, then Heaven's dimensions open up to us and we are granted the faculty to fight and to judge with Him. That is why after the wedding supper of the Lamb John sees the open Heavens and Jesus on His white horse.

Revelation 19:11-17

> *And I saw **Heaven opened**, and behold, a white horse; and He that sat upon him was called Faithful and True, and in righteousness He doth judge and make war.*
>
> *His eyes were as a flame of fire, and on His head were many crowns; and He had a name written that no man knew, but He Himself.*
>
> *And He was clothed with a vesture dipped in blood, and His name is called, THE WORD OF GOD.*
> *And the armies which were in Heaven, clothed in fine linen white and clean, followed Him upon white horses.*
>
> *And out of His mouth goeth a sharp sword with which He shall smite the nations, and He shall rule them with a rod of iron; and He treadeth the wine press of the fierceness and wrath of Almighty God.*

APOCALYPSE The Revelation of Jesus Christ

> *And He hath on His vesture and on His thigh a name written:* **KING OF KINGS, AND LORD OF LORDS.**
>
> *And I saw an angel standing in the sun, and he cried with a loud voice, saying to all the fowls that fly in the midst of heaven, "Come and gather yourselves together unto the supper of the great God.*
>
> *Revelation 19:11-17*

Jesus will not receive the name *"The Word of God"* or the title of His Reign sometime in the future. He has already been crowned King of Kings and Lord of Lords and He is already on Earth fighting our battles and establishing His justice over the Earth.

There are individual judgments over men and there are judgments over cities and nations. The judgments of God will not be all at once in one single day. God has been judging the nations forever and this becomes obvious throughout history.

When in Scripture it talks about horses ridden by men it symbolizes the strength and pride of men. In this case Jesus rides the horse, which speaks about the Authority and the Power He has given to His spouse.

Jesus in His white horse represents the union of His Spirit with ours. We are the white horse, redeemed and sanctified He can direct with the reins of His wisdom to execute justice along with Him.

Dr. Ana Méndez Ferrell

Mine anger was kindled against the shepherds, and I punished the goats: for the LORD of hosts hath visited his flock the house of Judah, and hath made them as his goodly horse in the battle.
Zechariah 10:3

Revelation 19:1-6

And after these things I heard a great voice of a multitude of people in Heaven, saying, "Alleluia! Salvation and glory and honor and power, unto the Lord our God, for true and righteous are His judgments: He hath judged the great whore who corrupted the earth with her fornication, and hath avenged the blood of His servants at her hand."

And again they said, "Alleluia!" And her smoke rose up for ever and ever.
And the four and twenty elders and the four living beings fell down and worshiped God who sat on the throne, saying, "Amen! Alleluia!"

And a voice came out of the throne, saying, "Praise our God, all ye His servants, and ye that fear Him, both small and great."

And I heard, as it were, the voice of a great multitude, and the voice of many waters, and the voice of mighty thunderings, saying, **"Alleluia! For the Lord God Omnipotent reigneth.**

Revelation 19:1-6

The Church, who is His wife, knows how to legislate in the Heavens to bring justice and judgment to Earth. It's an intercessory Church who cries out for Justice and also for Salvation and Mercy. She knows the beating of the Father's heart and joins Him so His judgments are carried out. She rejoices in knowing Him as sovereign King and righteous Judge. She rides with Him in battle to establish His Kingdom upon the Earth.

One of the things God is restoring in our lifetime is the establishment of His System of Justice over the Earth. Every kingdom needs to have a Supreme Court of Justice, and God also has one indeed. I will talk about this when we study the 24 Elders of the **Book of Revelation**.

10. BABYLON, THE GREAT HARLOT

1. Trained To Tear Down Babylon

From the onset of His message in the ***Book of Revelation***, Jesus is directing the prophecy into a climax, which is the judgment of *Babylon* - the great harlot - and of the corrupt systems of this world. To do this He has to refine the Church with the necessary enlightenment and tools to confront and subject her.

The first century Church was living under the conditions narrated in the 7 letters, which were designed to encourage and prepare them for the Judgment that was to come between the years 66 and 70 (*see Appendix 2*). However, their living and eternal content is part of our divine *Kingdom Manual*.

Every judgment of God is just, and those who will be assigned to judge have to be purged from every *Babylon*ic alliance and practice so they are not judged jointly with her.

> *And I saw thrones and they that sat upon them, and judgment was given unto them.*
> *Revelation 20:4*

APOCALYPSE The Revelation of Jesus Christ

Do ye not know that the saints shall judge the world? And if the world shall be judged by you, are ye unworthy to judge the smallest matters? Know ye not that we shall judge angels? How much more, things that pertain to this life?

1 Corinthians 6:2-3

2. Patmos, Third Vision

I found myself at the place of the doors inside God's Heart when a man dressed in white garments appeared with me holding a little book in one of his hands and a key chain with many keys in the other. I asked who he was and why had he come, and he answered me: "*I am one of the prophets of the Most High and I have been given the keys to open the prophecy. Jesus is the Spirit of Prophecy and many Words have been closed up and it has been granted us as prophets to open them.*" He then opened the little book and handed me a key. When I touched his hand to take it, a very bright light lit up my eyes as if they had their own light and suddenly we were transported to a desert plain in the midst of which was a very prosperous city. Although we were at a distance, we could see what was happening inside of it in full detail.

The city had a grotesque and abominable queen living in her palace with her son and both had casts hexes and spells to ally themselves with all the powers of the kingdom of darkness. The greater principalities gave them strength to extend their empire. Kings and peoples from the four corners of the Earth would come to them; big and small were entered into covenant and made to drink from a chalice that would inebriate them and have them believe their lies.

Upon drinking it, they were immediately surrounded by shadows and these would speak to them at the same time covering their eyes and ears. They laughed and felt happy by reason of the beverage that affects their reasoning and gives them great dreams and visions and strengthens them.

Their empire filled the whole Earth and men would bring their wickedness as a tribute and by this it became progressively enlarged and became more powerful. Then an opening above the city appeared as what seemed to be a different heaven from the one we were in, it was like a black hole and it was horrendous.

In an instant, the prophet and I were there. This place was the same city but seen in another form. It no longer had the splendor and prosperity of the former one. It had turned into an enormous building in the shape of a dark and sinister pyramid; there were birds of prey and ravens everywhere. Inside and out there prisons filled with millions of persons. The city had sort of tentacles and highways that came out of it and reached thousands of cities arranged in a similar fashion. These were the spiritual cities of deep darkness that are above each of earth's metropoles.

Both above and below there were sort of planes, some would sink to a horrid depth and others appeared to be as different levels above.

I asked the prophet what those places were and where we were. He told me: *"This is the abominable city, the great harlot that has held the nations and the peoples captive. She captivates them through commerce in the region and politics."* He then added, *"Here the dimensions of the spirit are not like those on Earth where only one apparently solid existential plane in three dimensions is visible. There are many more dimensions here, like the ones you saw in Heaven, the multiple dimensions of the Most High."*

APOCALYPSE The Revelation of Jesus Christ

There were seven high mountains around the city, which were reflected in each of the different planes just like when you put one mirror in front of another. The roadways joined the mountains of the great city and these supplied them not only through these, but also from the seas, from hell, from the sins of men and from the celestial bodies.

We entered through the city gates which were cluttered with masonic and witchcraft symbols. There was a curtain at the entrance made of something like a liquid cloud; everyone who entered had to go through it. I saw millions of persons cross it, they came in chained and with yokes upon them. Others came so burdened by demons they could barely walk. As they cross, an aqueous, imperceptible mask that affected their whole reality comes over them and covers their faces. The mask enables them to feel good and view the abominable as precious. They called evil, good and good, evil yet they were nothing more than robots in a system.

Upon seeing this, I was afraid to cross over but the prophet then took one of his keys and extended it in front of the watery door that opened without touching us. I then noticed that a magnificent covering of light surrounded us. The prophet told me: *"Fear not for those who have the Spirit of Prophecy can cross through here without being touched. Jesus is the Truth and he who walks in it, walks in His Light."*

After crossing we entered a deep murk. Inside was like a city with streets and public squares but all over the inside were prisons at differing levels of depth and darkness. We walked a long way till we reached an avenue that led to one of the mountains. The name of this mountain was *Religion* and the avenue was *Jezebel*, an enormous demon was guarding it and directing the people towards the mountain. There were many dining areas along the avenue where people delighted themselves in getting fat. Some never reached the mountain instead they fell into the abyss where they continued getting fat and worshipped a horrible demon whose appearance was like that of a toad whose skin overflowed with food of all sorts, it was the spirit of *gluttony* that served the *queen prostitute* next to the other two toads. One was *mammon*, the god of riches, and the other was *pharmakeia,* the goddess of sorcery.

When we got to the mountain, I was impacted to see the sharp resemblance it had to The Mount of God I had seen in His Glory full of small mountains where all of them comprised Jesus.

The mountain here was a great pyramid and full of small pyramids. Each one had the name of a kingdom and the man was exalted at the summit. The pyramid was made of partition walls and each one was a prison, all of them grounded from a dark substance full of lettering. All of them were conformed to the image of the man at the summit and they all wore masks from the water cloud. They were continuously fed contaminated food but they perceived it as delicious due to the mask and because they yearned to be a pyramid.

Inside the prisons, everyone felt they were dying; they were thirsty and hungry but couldn't move from there because they were tormented by demons of fear and guilt. There were pyramids from all religions and unfortunately also from *Christianity*.

Then the prophet showed me something that filled me with great pain. We were facing the pyramids with Christians, children of God, and in the hands of every man at the summit was an oil lamp and many of them were *out*.

They spoke about Jesus; men and women called by God and anointed by God but they had allowed their names to grow more in their own lives than Jesus. People inside the prisons clamored their names and ran to them to ease their pains.

I wept because I saw us, millions of Christians there; either one way or another, we had been made captive to *Babylon*'s system. I also saw myself; I was on a throne judging others and covered by the filthiness of my own righteousness.

When I saw myself, I fell prostrate before Jesus in deep repentance. I then saw a vision within a vision and I was taken to another place for a moment. Jesus wanted to show me what would give me the standard to never again judge others and to begin my own exit out of *Babylon*.

I found myself facing a gigantic mouth as of a whale. From inside it a force would come out and suck me to the inside while I was crying out the name of Jesus. Suddenly, the force stopped and I heard the voice of the Lord speaking like thunder: ***"Tell me what is more powerful than death and fear?"*** "I don't know Lord, I don't know" I answered Him trembling.

Then He told me: ***"It's temptation!"*** He then added: ***"If you are still standing it's because of my Grace. I know the heart of every man and if I had you face that which you could not overcome, you would fall like the rest of them. All men can fall into the same abomination, no one is better than the next,. If they have not fallen it is because of My Grace, it's because of My Love which sustains them."***

I clearly understood how all of us can err and fall, even having the best of intentions, we fall victims of *Babylon*. I began a process in which I asked God to show me how much of *Babylon* was in me, and how to exit that system which kills the life of God within us.

I returned from that vision to the city where the prophet was waiting for me. At that moment The Voice of The Father was heard saying: *"The doors of* Babylon *are open to allow all of those who hear My Voice to leave. I am calling out from My Holy Mountain:* Come out from there, MY PEOPLE! *Only those who humble themselves can exit. Only those who love My Name more than theirs can see the way out. Many of them touched my heart deeply as they clamored for their cities and their nations. I have next to me a flask filled with their tears and each one is a treasure to me. But when I raised them up and gave them a name, they extolled themselves and formed a kingdom for themselves, they laid down laws I did not give them and they appropriated my flock. They were imprisoned by* Babylon *who gave them a name to be recognized among the nations. Their lamps have not extinguished by reason of my love but not much time is left."*

While this was being said I remembered something I heard inside the Father's Heart, in that place which is like the Holy of Holies where all the wounds against Love are. His heart festered with an intense pain coming from a sore that bled incessantly, my body cramped just by looking at it. There and then I heard the voice of the Holy Spirit telling me: *"My people have gotten so accustomed in saying: 'I am from such a church, or from apostle Joe Blow, or from the so-and-so-network, or from this denomination or the other', which seems as something normal, permissible and even blessed by Me when this is an abomination that hurts Me deeply."* The Father then said: ***"I will not put up with this anymore."***

I cried a lot because I am guilty of those wounds. However, ever since that day I decided to dedicate my life to love and do whatever is required so God sees His Church united by the bonds of the Spirit and free from the system that separates and destroys us.

The theme of *Babylon* is a book in itself this being the whole structure of the kingdom of darkness making it impossible for me to break it down in one single chapter.

3. Who is Babylon?

The visions speak for themselves. *Babylon* is the religious system that kills the spiritual life of the Church and renders us inept to reign. *Babylon* exists ever since the religious systems exist, whichever these may be. This is the spirit that took over the Jewish priesthood during the time of Jesus and caused the fall of the ancient system. *Babylon* is not the Catholic Church as some think, it is a whole system that has the form of godliness yet lacks the life of God, "*The form*" will always resist *Life* and end up destroying it. It is a hypocritical system that says one thing and lives another.

Jesus speaks in an imperative manner to HIS PEOPLE to exit *Babylon*:

> *And I heard another voice from heaven saying, "Come out of her, my people, lest you share in her sins, and lest you receive of her plagues."*

Revelation 18:4

He is not speaking to a pagan people, He is talking to His Church. We all come from Babylon; nobody escapes. Those of us, who come from the Roman Church, come impregnated with religion. We exchange idolatry for the richness of the Bible but continue calling the rock and cement buildings where we gather: "church" and even "temple".

We went into the reformation principles Luther left us without realizing he also came from the Roman Babylonic system. He gave us the essence of the message of salvation we now have, but brought with it the same system of having church that jails us within the four walls of a building and little by little does away with the life of the true Church.

We continue using phrase such as *"See you in church on Sunday." "I am from apostle Joe Schmoe's church"* or *"...from pastor Joe Blow."* In other words: ***"I am from Paul and the other one from Apollos."*** *"My church is named such and such,"* or *"These are my sheep and these are from so and so's."* What are we doing? Jesus never ever gave us the option for the Church to belong to us.

Babylon makes us follow man under the guise of following God. We continue viewing the leadership as the anointed ones who are closer to God than the rest of the people. We continue separating the priests from the laymen. People depend more on the hand of man than that of God. They make the man or woman of God the source of their answers. As leaders, we do not propel people to depend on God and to know Him because in a certain way, we like them to depend on us. And unintentionally, whereas our words speak of loving God and following Him, our religious system makes us continue perpetuating their depending on us. If we are Heaven's Ambassadors, we need to speak, to see ourselves and manifest Heaven and not only reproduce men's systems.

When God revealed Himself to me. He showed me how much *Babylon* was in me. He allowed me to see how much I enjoyed man's reverence and being the great woman of God for my nation even though it was done unconsciously. He made me to understand how each one of us has collaborated in dividing the

Body of Christ and how this is nothing else but the *Babylon*ic System we operate in. When I understood this, I called out to His name to get me out of *Babylon* and help me get others out.

My message is not to get people out of churches but to get the churches out of *Babylon* along with all their people. People come to Jesus but they never destroy the *Babylon*ic structure from whence they have come throughout their generations. It's easier to attend a worship service on Sunday than to take authority and become the kings and priests He wants us to be. This system only has space for a few people to grow and evolve, but The Kingdom of God is not like that, everyone can become what God designed for them to be.

4. The Effects Of Babylon On Today's Church

a) *Babylon* is confusion and always twists God's message. Its main intent is to always separate Heaven from Earth and this will deny and obstruct the Heavenly reality inside the believer. Jesus came to join Heaven and Earth and give us the fullness of His life so we could truly be His body on Earth. The religious structures upon which we place divine revelation must be destroyed if we want the authority to reign.

b) *Babylon* calls itself "*Queen, Mistress of the Kingdoms.*" She wants to have the kingdom so Jesus doesn't have it. This causes people to not recognize Christ in His Kingdom, they receive Him as their Savior but not as the Sovereign One over their lives. It enables them to see Christ filled with His Glory in Heaven above yet the Christ who lives in their hearts as incapable of healing a cold **and solve their problems**. *Babylon* has to have control over everything and will never release it to the Holy Spirit.

The church deceived by *Babylon*, moans for God to descend His glory upon her. They fast and pray waiting for Him to one day send the revolving fire of His Glory that will usher in the awaited revival.

Beloved of My Father: Do we not realize that it's Jesus in all His Glory who inhabits us? What different, most powerful Glory can come than the one Jesus has already granted us?

"And the glory that You gave Me I have given them, that they may be one just as We are one"
John 17:22

Do you realize how this spirit comes to confound and rob us from the Glory Jesus already gave us?

In the **Book of Revelation**, Jesus reveals Himself to John in His Glory because it's in the midst of it that we can identify *Babylon* and come out of it. I am not saying that we need to leave the congregations, I am saying that whole congregations need to come out of *Babylon* and become re-structured to God's model: a Church united by the Holy Spirit, blessing and spiritually governing over the cities.

It's in that Glory that Jesus gives the Message to the seven churches, our Manual to enter the most powerful authority to govern with Jesus.

This message is not addressed to the observance of the commandments of the Old Covenant, instead it denounces the religious *Babylon*ic spirit and the manner it operates; it stealthily creeps up in the life of the believer robbing him/her of the life and of the fire of their first love until it leaves them without any authority or power.

11. VICTORY OVER *BABYLON*

1. The 7 Letters to the Churches: The Keys to Our Government

Although this is not one of the main themes that reveal the interpretation into the ***Book of Revelation***, I'll include it here as the *Victory over Babylon*. Each letter is a key that will allow us to defeat the *spirit of religion*.

Jesus manifests His own characteristics in each letter which help us obtain the prize that will allow us to govern, these are doors of infinite revelation to reign in the here and now.

A. The Church of Ephesus

> "To the angel of the church of Ephesus write, 'These things says He who holds the seven stars in His right hand, who walks in the midst of the seven golden lampstands:
> "I know your works, your labor, your patience, and that you cannot bear those who are evil. And you have tested those who say they are apostles and are not, and have found them liars; and you have persevered and have patience, and have labored for My name's sake and have not become weary.

APOCALYPSE The Revelation of Jesus Christ

> *Nevertheless I have this against you, that you have left your first love.*
>
> *Remember therefore from where you have fallen; repent and do the first works, or else I will come to you quickly and remove your lampstand from its place—unless you repent. But this you have, that you hate the deeds of the Nicolaitans, which I also hate.*
>
> *"He who has an ear, let him hear what the Spirit says to the churches. To him who overcomes I will give to eat from the Tree of Life, which is in the midst of the Paradise of God."*
>
> *Revelation 2:1-7*

Ephesians: Its name means "*Desirable.*" The theme of this letter is: **True Love is what Crowns Us.** Jesus introduces Himself to us as the "One who is amidst the candlesticks." Jesus is the One who is in control of the Church and not man. Pure love is what positions us in the center of Paradise, which is the place of ruling. Love is the *fountain of life* that feeds the nations and opposes *Nicolaitianism,* the hierarchical religious system that raises leadership atop a pedestal and takes the power and authority away from the lay people who are also children of God. *Nicolaitianism* raises its own kingdom and does not let God build His up. It steers the believers to depend on men who are at the head and not on THE HEAD who is Jesus. Although an order of authority exists in the Church, our spiritual dependence must be on Jesus.

Christ is the *Tree of Life*; this represents the life of the Spirit as opposed to the *Tree of Good and Evil,* which is based on human reasoning. The first one raises a system of life whereas the second, one of death. Love and our marriage commitment to Christ lead us to the dominion of all things.

B. The Church of Smyrna

> *"And to the angel of the church in Smyrna write, 'These things says the First and the Last, who was dead, and came to life:*
>
> *"I know your works, tribulation, and poverty (but you are rich); and I know the blasphemy of those who say they are Jews and are not, but are a synagogue of satan. Do not fear any of those things which you are about to suffer. Indeed, the devil is about to throw some of you into prison, that you may be tested, and you will have tribulation ten days. Be faithful until death, and I will give you the crown of life.*
>
> *"He who has an ear, let him hear what the Spirit says to the churches. He who overcomes shall not be hurt by the second death."*
>
> *Revelation 2:8-11*

Smyrna: Its name means "***Martyr***" or "***Fragrance***" Its theme is: **The Keys against Death.** Jesus introduces Himself as the First and the Last, the One who is alive but was dead. Jesus was the One who defeated death, the beginning and the end of all things. This is the key to vanquish death and to inherit the *Crown of Life*. We have to remain faithful unto death for this one: die to this world to live in Jesus. When we are able to see death as a victory and when we are clothed with our heavenly house, death cannot intimidate us. It's in this victory that we conquer the authority to resurrect the dead and transform dead territories so they can live. Having death under our feet enables us to defeat the devil in all his ways.

> *And they overcame him by the blood of the Lamb and by the word of their testimony, and they loved not their lives unto the death.*
> *Revelation 12:11*

> *I am crucified with Christ, nevertheless I live; yet not I, but Christ liveth in me. And the life which I now live in the flesh, I live by the faith of the Son of God, who loved me and gave Himself for me.*
> *Galatians 2:20*

This key gives us the ability to understand how tribulations are instruments that position us more and more into greater higher authority ranks.

To vanquish death in all its forms: *fear, sicknesses, bitterness* and *sin*, enables us to live in the spheres of what is Eternal.

This key changes our perspective to see things from their temporary state to see them in their Eternal function and purpose.

C. The Church of Pergamos

> *"And to the angel of the church in Pergamos write, 'These things says He who has the sharp two-edged sword:*
>
> *"I know your works, and where you dwell, where satan's throne is. And you hold fast to My name, and did not deny My faith even in the days in which Antipas was My faithful martyr, who was killed among you, where satan dwells. But I*

> *have a few things against you, because you have there those who hold the doctrine of Balaam, who taught Balak to put a stumbling block before the children of Israel, to eat things sacrificed to idols, and to commit sexual immorality. Thus you also have those who hold the doctrine of the Nicolaitans, which thing I hate. Repent, or else I will come to you quickly and will fight against them with the sword of My mouth.*
>
> *"He who has an ear, let him hear what the Spirit says to the churches. To him who overcomes I will give some of the hidden manna to eat. And I will give him a white stone, and on the stone a new name written which no one knows except him who receives it."*
>
> *Revelation 2:12 -17*

Pergamos: Its name means *"High Place"* and its theme is **The Power of the Word.** Jesus introduces Himself as the One who has the two edged sword; Jesus is the One who releases Judgment with the authority of His Word. Those who govern with Him must have authority to judge and see all things from God's righteous Heart. We have to tower above the obscure levels of our own opinion to judge with righteous judgment.

This is the key to conquer every circumstance even if it's satan's throne on Earth. It's the key to overcome the power of greed, money and the desire to be in good standing with men than with God.

Balaam, the prophet was mentioned in this letter. He sold his message and his call for money, as nowadays there are those who do so too. To eat things sacrificed to idols and commit fornication speaks to us about how the Word of God is spoken with indolence and lukewarmness. This attitude is contrary to the sharp two-edged sword, which confronts and discerns the soul and the spirit, thereby converting the heart.

The prize is the *hidden manna,* the true revelation necessary to rule. It is the provision of Heaven that comes over the givers, those who divest themselves of their wealth for the love of God's work and their fellow men, defeating *mammon,* the god of the riches.

God gives us *a new name* here; our authority and our identity are in that name. Through this *new name* we can subdue nations, loose the loins of kings, straighten crooked places, open iron gates, and receive from God His treasures.

> *Thus saith the LORD to His anointed, to Cyrus, whose right hand I have held to* **subdue nations before him***; and I will* **loose the loins of kings** *to open before him the two leaved gates; and the gates shall not be shut: I will go before thee, and make the crooked places straight; I will break in pieces the gates of brass, and cut in sunder the bars of iron. And I will give thee* **the treasures of darkness** *and* **hidden riches of secret places***, that thou mayest know that I, the LORD, who* **call thee by thy name***, am the God of Israel.*
>
> Isaiah 45:1-3

D. The Church of Thyatira

> *"And to the angel of the church in Thyatira write, 'These things says the Son of God, who has*

eyes like a flame of fire, and His feet like fine brass:

"I know your works, love, service, faith, and your patience; and as for your works, the last are more than the first.

Nevertheless I have a few things against you, because you allow that woman Jezebel, who calls herself a prophetess, to teach and seduce My servants to commit sexual immorality and eat things sacrificed to idols. And I gave her time to repent of her sexual immorality, and she did not repent.

Indeed I will cast her into a sickbed, and those who commit adultery with her into great tribulation, unless they repent of their deeds.
I will kill her children with death, and all the churches shall know that I am He who searches the minds and hearts. And I will give to each one of you according to your works.

"Now to you I say, and to the rest in Thyatira, as many as do not have this doctrine, who have not known the depths of satan, as they say, I will put on you no other burden. But hold fast what you have till I come.

And he who overcomes, and keeps My works until the end, to him I will give power over the nations —

"He shall rule them with a rod of iron;

They shall be dashed to pieces like the potter's vessels'—as I also have received from My Father; and I will give him the morning star.

"He who has an ear, let him hear what the Spirit says to the churches."

Revelation 2:18-29

Thyatira: It´s name is uncertain; its true meaning is unknown. Its theme is: **The Key that discerns what comes from God and what comes from man.** In this letter Jesus introduces Himself as the One Who has *eyes like fire* and *feet like fine brass*.

This key is the one that determines the authority to rule nations. To govern is to judge and execute righteousness but it has to be according to the *Eyes of God*. He sees each one of our actions from different angles. We see the facts in black and white; this is *the Tree of Good and Evil*. The Eyes of God analyze every circumstance that surrounds each case, the extenuating and the aggravating.

> *...and shall make Him of quick understanding in the fear of the LORD; and He shall not judge after the sight of His eyes, neither reprove after the hearing of His ears. But with righteousness shall He judge the poor, and reprove with equity for the meek of the earth; and He shall smite the earth with the rod of His mouth, and with the breath of His lips shall He slay the wicked.*
>
> *Isaiah 11:3-4*

Jezebel is the *authority-usurping spirit*, the one who seeks her own kingdom above God's; the one that judges through the limited and inquisitor eyes of religion, the one who governs through principles of fear, intimidation and control over people. She does not allow them to depend on God but forces them to depend on man, making God's children spiritually crippled. Her messages are attractive for the soul but lack commitment to God.

Jezebel leads to fornication. In the spiritual sense this is to please oneself with the warmth of a relationship without the commitment of a marriage; this is to try to endeavor moments of intimacy with the Holy Spirit without a real determination and covenant to follow Jesus wherever He goes. We see this clearly explained in Chapter 14 in the **Book of Revelation** where the 144,000 chosen are described and how they do not spiritually defile themselves and achieve it through their total commitment to Jesus.

> *These are they are who are not defiled with women **(Jezebel)**, for they are virgins **(Consecrated)**. These are they that follow the Lamb whithersoever He goeth. These were redeemed from among men, being the first fruits unto God and to the Lamb.*
>
> *Revelation 14:4 (emphasis added by the author)*

Jezebel is not only *a spirit* but also *a doctrine* where the eyes of men are diverted and focus on man instead than on God. "*To know the depths of satan*" has to do with entering into intimacy with him, making pacts with his tricks and seductions. We must have understanding on the strategies and works of the devil but without getting involved with him.

Fear of man and *his dominion over others* is the essence of a religious system, which shrewdly disguises itself as "*godliness*" and is difficult to identify. This is why Jesus manifests Himself with *Eyes of Fire* so through Him we can see its fraudulent works of darkness, cloaked in their false light.

> *… having a form of godliness but denying the power thereof. From such turn away.*
> *2 Timothy 3:5*

Religiosity is the toughest mountain hindering us from governing with Christ. To him that overcomes, Jesus gives them authority over the nations.

Jesus broke the religious system of His time with an iron rod and to him who overcomes religion He gives this same authority. He also manifests Himself in this letter as the *bright morning star* in our lives.

> *We have also a more sure word of prophecy, unto which ye do well that ye take heed, as unto a light that shineth in a dark place, until the day dawn and the **day star arise in your hearts.***
> 2 Peter 1:19

This is the shining glow that becomes visible of Christ incarnate in every believer when the vessel that contains Him has conformed to His Word. The vessel and the Word are, and walk in agreement.

If the seven Churches form the Candlestick of the Light of God, Thyatira would be at the center as a vital government message.

E. The Church of Sardis

> *"And to the angel of the church in Sardis write, "These things says He who has the seven Spirits of God and the seven stars: 'I know your works, that you have a name that you are alive, but you are dead.*
> *Be watchful, and strengthen the things which remain, that are ready to die, for I have not found your works perfect before God.*

> *Remember therefore how you have received and heard; hold fast and repent. Therefore if you will not watch, I will come upon you as a thief, and you will not know what hour I will come upon you.*
>
> *You have a few names even in Sardis who have not defiled their garments; and they shall walk with Me in white, for they are worthy.*
>
> *He who overcomes shall be clothed in white garments, and I will not blot out his name from the Book of Life; but I will confess his name before My Father and before His angels.*
>
> *"He who has an ear, let him hear what the Spirit says to the churches."'*
>
> *Revelation 3:1-6*

Sardis: Its name means *"Prince of Joy"*. Its theme is: **The Key to Know the Multiple Manifestations of the Spirit and of the Angels that are Granted to us.** Jesus introduces Himself as the One who has the seven Spirits of God and the seven stars.

He, whose life is not immersed in Him, will eventually die off possessing a name of one who lives but being indeed dead. This key requires of a holiness that can only be obtained by knowing God every day and fusing evermore with Him. His seven Spirits are the ones who reveal Him and give Life to the Church. Our growth with Him depends on our knowing Him in each one of these seven characteristics.

> *And the **Spirit of the LORD** shall rest upon Him--the **Spirit of wisdom and understanding**, the Spirit of counsel and*

> *might, the Spirit of knowledge and of the fear of the LORD."*
>
> Isaiah 11:2

We see this passage in **Isaiah** how the manifestations of the Seven Spirits are key to govern with righteous judgments. However, these in turn broaden, as we understand their functions.

> ***The Spirit of the Lord GOD*** *is upon Me, because the LORD hath anointed Me **to preach** good tidings unto the meek. He hath sent me to **bind up the brokenhearted**, to proclaim **liberty to the captives**, and the opening of the prison to them that are bound, To proclaim the **acceptable year of the LORD**, and the day of vengeance of our God; to **comfort** all that mourn, To appoint unto them that mourn in Zion, to give unto them beauty for ashes, the oil of **joy for mourning,** the garment of praise for the spirit of heaviness, that they might be called trees of righteousness, the planting of the LORD, that He might be glorified." And they shall **build the wastes of old**, they shall raise up the former desolations, and they shall **repair the waste cities**, the desolations of many generations.*
>
> Isaiah 61:1-4

To govern with Christ refers to all those things that lead to restoration and to the re-building of that which was lost.

Jesus rules with His angels and He has granted them to co-labor alongside us. All throughout the **Book of Revelation** we see the angels interacting with the believers and with John to the point that the apostle calls them *"fellow servants"*.

It's through our contact with the Holy Spirit and The Fear of God that we remain in holiness, robed in white raiment and endure in the life of God.

It's in this key that God grants us, apart from being robed in white raiment and our names inscribed in the Book of Life, for our names to be confessed before the Father and His angels.

There is major authority here. When our names resonate inside the Father, angels rush to our aid. The angels know those sealed by the Father.

> *... For He shall give His angels charge over thee to keep thee in all thy ways, they shall bear thee up in their hands, lest thou dash thy foot against a stone. Thou shalt tread upon the lion and adder; the young lion and the dragon shalt thou trample underfoot...Because he hath set his love upon Me, therefore will I deliver him; I will set him on high, because he hath known My name."*
>
> *Psalm 91:11-14*

F. The Church of Philadelphia

> *"And to the angel of the church in Philadelphia write, "These things says He who is holy, He who is true, 'He who has the key of David, He who opens and no one shuts, and shuts and no one opens":*
> *"I know your works. See, I have set before you an open door, and no one can shut it; for you have a little strength, have kept My word, and have*

APOCALYPSE The Revelation of Jesus Christ

not denied My name. Indeed I will make those of the synagogue of satan, who say they are Jews and are not, but lie—indeed I will make them come and worship before your feet, and to know that I have loved you.

Because you have kept My command to persevere, I also will keep you from the hour of trial which shall come upon the whole world, to test those who dwell on the earth. Behold, I am coming quickly! Hold fast what you have, that no one may take your crown.

He who overcomes, I will make him a pillar in the temple of My God, and he shall go out no more. I will write on him the name of My God and the name of the city of My God, the New Jerusalem, which comes down out of heaven from My God. And I will write on him My new name.

"He who has an ear, let him hear what the Spirit says to the churches."'

Revelation 3:7-13

Philadelphia: Its name means ***"Fraternal Love"*** its theme is: **The Key of David.** Jesus displays Himself as Holy and True. He has the keys of David, that open and no one shuts, and shuts, and no one opens.

Indeed all who delight in piety and are determined to live a devoted and godly life in Christ Jesus will meet with persecution [will be made to suffer because of their religious stand].

2 Timothy 3:12 Amplified Bible[15]

---

[15] *2 Tim. 3:12 Indeed all who delight in piety and are determined to live a devoted and godly life in Christ Jesus will meet with persecution [will be made to suffer because of their religious stand].*

Dr. Ana Méndez Ferrell

...if we suffer, we shall also reign with Him.
2 Timothy 2:12

The Kingdom is given to us through our overcoming tribulation and persecution. The devil wants to shut all doors on us but the One who has the keys to open and shut is Jesus and not satan.

Once more, *The Keys of The Kingdom* are handed over to us through Christ revealing Himself in our lives, which causes the gates of Hades not to prevail against the Kingdom children.

Jesus reveals Himself here as Holy and Truthful. To live conformed to His Holiness and to His Truth is what will always keep the doors open for us to do the work of God and to establish His Kingdom.

Truth is immovable; all that is false and illusory inevitably ends up shattered at the feet of Truth. Remaining in Truth makes all systems around us begin to topple. Because lies and falsehood cannot stand Truth, they will persecute it unto death as they did with Jesus but at the end Truth resurrects and triumphs.

One day I had a vision and saw Moses standing in front of the *Red Sea*. His rod represented the Word of Truth that Jehovah had given him: "**He shall deliver His people**." Moses stood holding his rod up high until everything began to shake, the winds became stronger and the waters could no longer remain in their place and had to open up. Then I heard the Lord say: *Heaven and Earth shall pass away but the Word of the Lord remains forever.*

To stand on the Truth at whatever the cost shall always open doors, seas, form pathways in rugged places, part mountains, shut lion's mouths and shatter hell's gates. This is one of the Most High's great keys of government.

Truth and Holiness are God's fortified castle, the walls and the columns that support it.

Columns are a symbol of the foundation of what has been established to support the building. They imply strength, rectitude, and composure. In the natural, this is what keeps the house stable and the most secure place amidst an earthquake.

> *And he raised up the pillars before the temple, one on the right hand and the other on the left, and called the name of that one on the right hand Jachin [that is, He shall establish], and the name of that on the left Boaz [that is, In it is strength].*
> *2 Chronicles 3:17 Amplified*

To live and express His Holiness and Truth is not mimicking it but allowing Him to produce it in us. When He encounters vessels where He is free to manifest Who He is, He will place in them His greatest prize, they will carry the Name of God on their foreheads and will genuinely be the Heavenly City walking on Earth.

G. The Church of Laodicea

> *"And to the angel of the church of the Laodiceans write, 'These things says the Amen, the Faithful and True Witness, the Beginning of the creation of God:*
> *"I know your works, that you are neither cold nor hot. I could wish you were cold or hot.*
> *So then, because you are lukewarm, and neither cold nor hot, I will vomit you out of My mouth.*
> *Because you say, "I am rich, have become wealthy, and have need of nothing' — and do not know that you are wretched, miserable, poor, blind, and naked*

— I counsel you to buy from Me gold refined in the fire, that you may be rich; and white garments, that you may be clothed, that the shame of your nakedness may not be revealed; and anoint your eyes with eye salve, that you may see.

As many as I love, I rebuke and chasten. Therefore be zealous and repent.

Behold, I stand at the door and knock. If anyone hears My voice and opens the door, I will come in to him and dine with him, and he with Me.

To him who overcomes I will grant to sit with Me on My throne, as I also overcame and sat down with My Father on His throne.

"He who has an ear, let him hear what the Spirit says to the churches."

Revelation 3:14-22

Laodicea: Sit at God's Throne with Jesus.

Jesus introduces Himself as the Amen, the True and Faithful Witness, the Beginning of the Creation.

The challenge here is to defeat religion at one of its most important disguises, which are the external appearances; to say one thing and live a different reality blinded and thinking we possess it all because of superficial success. Jesus manifests Himself as the Amen and trains us not to be double-faced but to live the certainty of everything He is.

The government key here is to become an experiential witness of Heaven. To see and hear what The Kingdom of God says and does is pivotal to reigning in the spiritual spheres.

Jesus manifests Himself as the *Beginning of all Creation* because all things were created precisely from the realm of the Spirit. To penetrate His invisible Kingdom, to hear and see Jesus and the Father is what truly makes us witnesses. As we previously saw the Spirit of Prophecy is the testimony of Jesus. It's through understanding and continually entering the Spirit that we will receive the salve to see as God sees. Our fellowship with God and our longing of becoming clothed with Jesus will form in us our true raiment, which is our heavenly house.

To see ourselves as He sees us is the mirror that confronts us to die to all that is worldly and in this manner His fire purifies us as gold.

The Lord's Supper is the greatest inheritance He left us, through it we are transformed to His image to sit with Him in His Throne and reign with Him in the here and the now.[16]

This letter is not a call to salvation but to reign; to allow Him to take the throne and government of our lives to make us kings and priests unto God the Father.

---

[16] *The book "Eat of my Flesh and Drink of My Blood" shares in depth on the riches of the Lord's Supper.*

12. THE MESSIAH'S KINGDOM

1. A Spiritual Kingdom

This is our seventh interpretation theme. In chapter 7 we spoke about the *Power* and the *Purpose* of our *Messiah's First Coming*. Now we are going further to understand how that marvelous Kingdom He brought us manifests on Earth.

During Jesus' time the people of Israel expected the Messiah to sit on *Jerusalem's* political throne. When He didn't and thereby establishing that His Kingdom was not of this world, many of the Jews who followed Him ended up disappointed, among them were Judas Iscariot the Zealots and most of the members of the Sanhedrin. This caused them to eliminate Jesus as the possible Messiah and continued waiting for the One who would fulfill this expectation. This idea still prevails and spurs the thinking of many to believe the Kingdom has not come. They yearned for a physical kingdom therefore they rejected the idea of an invisible one.

Jesus clearly told them how His Kingdom on Earth was to be:

> *Jesus answered, "My kingdom is not **of this world**. If My kingdom were **of this world**, My servants would fight, so that I should not be delivered to the Jews; but now My kingdom is not from here."*
>
> *John 18:36*

APOCALYPSE   The Revelation of Jesus Christ

Asked by the Pharisees when the Kingdom of God would come, He replied to them by saying, "The kingdom of God does not come with signs to be observed or with visible display, Nor will people say, Look! Here [it is]! or, See, [it is] there! For behold, the kingdom of God is within you [in your hearts] and **among you [surrounding you].***"*
Luke 17:20-21 Amplified

Even though The Kingdom of God is invisible, it has to impact the Earth through the sons of God and by the mighty hand of the Lord the results will be visible. The righteousness is going to be established, evil will be judged and the knowledge of God's manifested glory will cover the Earth as the waters cover the sea.

So let us carefully analyze this topic:

Jesus came to bring His Father's Kingdom and He did not fail in His mission. He is seated at the Father's right Hand, crowned as King of kings and Lord of lords governing together with His Church, which is His Bride. She is flesh of His flesh and bone of His bones and legitimately His body.

The Church has the authority from her Head who is Christ and has the victory over everything Jesus paid for her at the Cross of Calvary. She is the Heavenly City in the middle of which Jesus is providing for her all she needs.

From the beginning to the end of the Old Testament, Jesus, being the Spirit of Prophecy announces His coming in the flesh and the establishment of His Kingdom and does not separate one from the other. The coming of Messiah is the hub of God's message and our inheritance. To understand in depth the work of

Messiah we have to realize that He operates simultaneously in two dimensions, Heaven and Earth are united in Jesus and if He reigns in Heaven He does it on Earth too.

> *If then you were raised with Christ, seek those things which are above, where Christ is, sitting at the right hand of God.*[2] **Set your mind on things above, not on things on the earth.**
> *Colossians 3:1-2*

2. Patmos - Fourth Vision

Once again I found myself on the Mount from where milk and honey flow and from which new wine having an exquisite fragrance sprung forth. I was delighting myself facing the clear water fountain filled with lights that descended forming a great river that flooded the valley.

I then saw many other mounts flowing out from the great Mount; waters of life, honey and new wine flowed forth from each one and filled the Heaven as far as my eye could see.[17]

Altogether with the great Mount, they conformed Jesus and came from Jesus as I had seen it the first time but this time, a new dimension opened underneath my feet.

From behind the great Mount, an intense Light stronger than the Sun's appeared and in the center of this light was One resembling the Son of God seated at His Throne. It was made of fire but different than the one on Earth; it blazed but it did not burn, it was as transparent and translucent as millions of lit sparkles. From its center a river of fire descended all the way to Earth.

---

[17] *Words that confirm this vision: Joel 3:18 and Zechariah 13:1*

Then the Great Mount descended and filled the whole Earth. A great joy came to Heaven and a majestic symphony overflowed it and the myriad of angels sang: Hallelujah, Hallelujah our God Almighty reigns!!

I then saw how the hillsides of the Mount formed what appeared to be a gold overlay which covered all the nations and I heard the voice of the Holy Spirit, that said: "***Herein, the Tabernacle of God with men.***"

I saw how the river of fire that came from the throne of Jesus was poured over the heads of many people and these converted into mounts. I then heard how a voice came out from the fire and when they heard it, the mounts grew taller and stronger.

And the river of fire is never quenched because it had been established for Eternity.

3. Mount Zion is The Seat of His Government

From the place I was at, I was able to understand everything with great clarity and knew what I was watching was the day the Holy Spirit was poured over all flesh. The Holy Mountain of God was established on that day. The devils' government was defeated on that day and the One who has the keys of death and hell is Jesus Christ.

The passage of Daniel when he sees the Rock coming out of Heaven and destroys the image that symbolizes the *Babylon*ic empire came to mind:

> *Then the iron, the clay, the bronze, the silver, and the gold were crushed together, and became like chaff from the summer threshing floors; the wind carried them away so that no trace of them was found. And the stone that struck the image became **a great mountain and filled the whole earth.***
>
> Daniel 9:35

> *The mount of Zion is over the Earth and it is the government of God that was established once and for all. But you have come **to Mount Zion** and to the city of the living God, the heavenly Jerusalem, to an innumerable company of angels.*
>
> Hebrew 12:22

His Kingdom is invisible and it's in the midst of us. The issue is that the Church has not known how to enter and live in it because they have evolved poorly into the realm of the Spirit. Besides, the placing of His Kingdom as a "future" manifestation, removes the possibility from the Church to enter into it **now**.

It's an indisputable reality for everyone that Jesus is in the midst of us as King of Kings and Lord of Lords and if we understand what this means in its fullness we will see the Church enter into its highest Glory manifestation.

There is a clear manifestation in the Bible of His coming in the spiritual sense, making His Tabernacle inside of us.

What we have to understand is that when Jesus spoke that He would come again to be with us, He never referred to a *Second Coming* in the flesh, coming to reign in Jerusalem, and most of time He was talking about His spiritual Presence among His church.

In this matter, it is very important to study the words Jesus spoke and where He spoke them.

As we have seen before, He said that it would not be in this manner.

To assume that there is a physical second coming, in which He comes to reign on Earth, as it is taught in the Evangelical Church, creates a problem that clashes against the very design of God.

Ask yourself this questions: If Christ would come to reign on the Earth, in a physical body, what would happen to His spiritual body that is the Church? Would we stop being His body? Would He have two bodies? Would we stop having comunion and intimacy with Him spiritually, and would we have to take a plane to go see Him?

Let's break down this concept in detail:
Most of the time when Jesus spoke about Him coming back, He was talking about His spiritual presence within us, His Church. In a physical manner as He was on Earth, He could not live in the hearts of the believers. He never made a call to His disciples to receive Him in their hearts, because that only happened the day of Pentecost.

In Section III of this book, I lay out the Greek words that determine the different ways He comes to us and how He himself describes His coming back.

This is why He said in ***John 14*** that it was convenient for Him to go and said how He would come again with His Father to make in us a dwelling place.

> *Jesus answered and said unto him, If a man love me, he will keep my words: and my Father will love him, and we will come unto him, and make our abode with him.*
>
> *John 14:23*

In most of the scriptures where His Second Coming is mentioned it's as four manifestations of The Word: **Parousia**, **Epifania, Apocalipsis** and **Erchomai**; have to do with His Presence in the Church as the *Temple of God* or as a *Manifestation of His Glory that judges evil.* **(see Instrument 1 in Section IV where I explain the meaning of each of these words.)**

Let's see an example of this:

> *And while they looked steadfastly toward heaven as He went up, behold, two men stood by them in white apparel, who also said, "Men of Galilee, why do you stand gazing up into heaven? This same Jesus, who was taken up from you into heaven, will so come (erchomai[18]) in like manner as you saw Him go into heaven."*
>
> **Acts 1:10-11**

A better translation using *the aorist form* would be: ... *This same Jesus, who was taken up from you into heaven "comes eternally" in like manner as you saw Him go into heaven.*

---

[18] *Erchomai, conjugated in a tense called Aorist: 1. A form of a verb in some languages, such as Classical Greek, that expresses action without indicating its completion or continuation., 2. A form of a verb in some languages, such as Classical Greek or Sanskrit, that in the indicative mood expresses past action. (Free Dictionary)*

After His ascension He appeared many times to Paul, and to John and for sure He did as well with the other Apostles. They "*saw Him again in His resurrected body*" when He came to them.

> *But rise, and stand upon thy feet: for I have appeared unto thee for this purpose, to make thee a minister and a witness both of these things which thou hast seen, and of those things in the which* **I will appear unto thee;**
>
> Acts 26:16

The other way in which Jesus spoke about Him coming back was a sign in the sky, as a lightening that was going to be so noticable, because He was going to destroy the city of Jerusalem and put and end to the Old System. These words were fulfilled during the fall of *Jerusalem* and the destruction of the Temple in the year 70. (*see Instrument 1 section IV*)

It is impossible to understand Jesus' prophecies about the end without reading the Jewish history in the first Century.

Flavio Josephus, a historian and a pharesee who lived in those days wrote in his work "*The War of the Jews*", everything that happened that brought the destruction of the former Israel. These writings give us light to see that every word that Jesus spoke to His people and His generation about the end, was fulfilled.[19]

To read *Matthew, Mark, Luke* and *John*, as if they were the New Covenant, and not the completion of all Scripture in Yeshua the Messiah of Israel, is the greatest mistake that has lead the Church to misinterpret everything Jesus said about the "END".

---

[19] *In instrument # 2 I make a synopsis of the writtings of Flavio Josepho. A much deeper research is found in my book "The End of an Era".*

I will continue to break down *The Return of Christ* in the following chapters since this requires a much deeper understanding.

4. The Purpose of The Messiah's Kingdom

The Kingdom purpose is the center of God's Heart and this is what fills the Earth with the KNOWLEDGE of the Glory of God as the waters cover the sea.

He will do this through a people who know Him and manifest Him *in every sphere of society*. People who understand they are kings and priests, having a mission as such among the nations.

We have to establish the Mount of God above *every* mount of influence on Earth: politics, economy, health, arts, media, movie industry, energy resources, space science, fashion, et cetera.

The Kingdom culture has to conquer every culture on Earth. We, the children of God, are not part of the Earth's culture nor is our citizenship of this world. We no longer belong here; we belong to Heaven.

To understand these things changes our way of thinking, and instead of waiting to escape from here and for the whole world to be destroyed, we begin to think on how to pray to win our nations so none are lost.

God wants to make us overcomers and make us shine thereby shaming the strong and the wise of this world. He wants to demonstrate to the devil His children are capable, through their redeemed humanity by Jesus, of destroying all his structures and plans of destruction.

13. THE ABODE OF GOD IN THE CLOUDS

1. The Clouds in the Kingdom of GOD

The majority of the theological currents, although not all of them, have always believed that Jesus will literally return in the midst of clouds. But what would happen if Scripture itself shows us that the clouds Jesus was referring to are not those puffy vapor masses that float in the sky?

Our understanding opens up when we see the intimate relationship existing between the abode of God and the clouds.

> *Dost thou know the (difference) balancings of the clouds, the wondrous works of Him who is perfect in knowledge?*
>
> *Job 37:16*

> *Not only that, but can anyone understand the spreadings of the clouds or the thundering noise of His tabernacle?*
>
> *Job 36:29*

> *He made darkness His secret place; His tabernacle round about Him was dark waters and thick clouds of the skies.*
>
> *Psalm 18:11*

> *Clouds and darkness are round about Him; righteousness and judgment are the habitation of His throne.*
>
> Psalm 97:2

> *who layeth the beams of His chambers in the waters, who maketh the clouds His chariot, who walketh upon the wings of the wind;*
>
> Psalm 104:3

God's manifestation in the clouds is not a single event as traditional theologies suggest: *He lives surrounded by them.*

Now that we have gained understanding about this, we're going to explore the deeper meaning of what Messiah wanted to make known to us.

Jesus clearly announced how He would come to dwell in the Spirit in the midst of His Church.

> *When the Son of Man shall come in His glory and all the holy angels with Him,* **then shall He sit upon the throne of His Glory,**
>
> Matthew 25:31

We see here that **His coming in the clouds is directly related with His sitting on the throne** and not with a physical coming. This is clear to us now that we have been studying the *Key Themes of Interpretation*.

Now: This is of **vital importance** because if Jesus is not yet seated at the Throne at the right hand of The Father then He is not King of Kings either.

Let's make it very clear: Jesus has already been crowned and this title has already been given to Him.

He declares to the high priest when this would happen:

> *Jesus said unto him, "Thou hast said; nevertheless I say unto you, **hereafter shall ye see** the Son of Man sitting at the right hand of Power, and coming in the clouds of heaven."*
>
> *Then the high priest rent his clothes, saying, "He hath spoken blasphemy! What further need have we of witnesses? Behold, now ye have **heard his blasphemy**!*
>
> *Matthew 26:64-65*

He told him: "***Hereafter*** *shall you see the Son of Man sitting at the right hand of the Power of God and coming in the clouds of heaven.*" He did not mean in two thousand years, "*Hereafter*" means from that moment on.

For the religious mind, this was considered blasphemy and for many whose preconceived ideas do not allow them to see this truth, they too will consider it blasphemy.

The prophet Daniel had a clear vision of the moment when Jesus was to take up the throne.

> *I saw in the night visions, and behold,* **one like the Son of Man came with the clouds of heaven**, *and came to the Ancient of Days, and they brought Him near before Him. And there was given Him dominion and glory and a Kingdom, that all people, nations, and languages should serve Him. His dominion is an everlasting dominion, which shall not pass away, and His Kingdom that which shall not be destroyed.*

> *...until the Ancient of Days came, and judgment was given to the saints of the Most High; and the time came that the saints possessed the Kingdom.*
>
> *But the judgment shall sit, and they shall take away (from the fourth beast) his dominion, to consume and to destroy it unto the end. And the kingdom and dominion, and the greatness of the kingdom under the whole heaven, shall be given to the people of the saints of the Most High, whose Kingdom is an everlasting Kingdom, and all dominions shall serve and obey Him.'*
>
> *Daniel 7:13-14, 22, 26-27*

Now, if Jesus has not yet received the Throne and The Father has not yet given us The Kingdom, then the Church has no power and remains in limbo, waiting, which makes no sense.

The author of Hebrews clearly stated that the Kingdom was *already* ours.

> *Therefore,* ***we receiving a Kingdom which cannot be moved****, let us have grace whereby we may serve God acceptably, with reverence and godly fear.*
>
> *Hebrews 12:28*

Next, these clouds the prophet Daniel talks about, have more to do with the covering that surrounds the throne of the Father than with the physical clouds.

Let's look at other cloud-concepts in the Word:

2. The Clouds are God's Tabernacle with Men

One of the words translated as 'cloud' in Hebrew is ***"anan"*** which means *'covering, or covered sky*[20]

> *Also, can any understand the spreadings of the clouds, or the thundering noise of His tabernacle ?*
>
> *Job 36:29*

> *It is He that sitteth upon the circle of the earth, and the inhabitants thereof are as grasshoppers, who stretcheth out the heavens as a curtain and spreadeth them out as a tent to dwell in.*
>
> *Isaiah 40:22*

The thundering noise of His tabernacle is the sound of His voice speaking in His dwelling place, which is the congregation of the saints. It's the sound of the cloud of witnesses that make up the eternal Temple throughout the ages, it's the sound of the multitude of the saints that make the waters of life flow through worship, each one a stream that joins the other to form the sound of many waters.

> *And I heard, as it were, the voice of a great multitude, and* **the voice of many waters, and the voice of mighty thunderings,** *saying, "Alleluia! For the Lord God Omnipotent reigneth.*
>
> *Revelation 19:6*

---

[20] 6051. NînDo{anan, aw-nawn'; from 6049; a cloud (as covering the sky), i.e. the nimbus or thunder-cloud:—cloud(-y).

APOCALYPSE The Revelation of Jesus Christ

*Therefore, seeing we also are compassed about by so great **a cloud of witnesses**, let us lay aside every weight, and the sin which doth so easily beset us, and let us run with patience the race that is set before us.*

Hebrews 12:1

The clouds represent the "***anan***" of God, His Grace covering that protects us.

He made darkness His secret place; His pavilion round about Him was dark waters and thick clouds of the skies.

Psalm 18:11

... who layeth the beams of His chambers in the waters, who maketh the clouds His chariot, who walketh upon the wings of the wind;

Psalm 104:3

The clouds are the place from where God speaks to His people. Not only in the Old Testament but also in the New; they are symbols of the prophetic manifestation of the Holy Spirit.

*While he was saying this, a **cloud** came and overshadowed them; and they were fearful as they entered the **cloud**. ^{35} And a voice came out of the cloud, saying, "This is My beloved Son, Hear Him!"*

Luke 9:34-35

And the LORD descended in the cloud and stood with him there, and proclaimed the name of the LORD.

Exodus 34:5

Then a cloud covered the tent of the congregation, and the glory of the LORD filled the tabernacle. And Moses was not able to enter into the tent of the congregation because the cloud abode thereon, and the glory of the LORD filled the tabernacle.
Exodus 40:34-35

When the "***anan***" covering of God is removed from over a place then the judgments of God are released.

And the heaven departed as a scroll when it is rolled together, and every mountain and island were moved out of their places.

And the kings of the earth, and the great men, and the rich men, and the chief captains, and the mighty men, and every bondman, and every free man, hid themselves in the dens and in the rocks of the mountains; and they said to the mountains and rocks,

"Fall on us, and hide us from the face of Him that sitteth on the throne, and from the wrath of the Lamb!

Revelation 6:14-16

This Scripture does not talk about the end of the world but about how His covering is removed so God's Righteousness is released over the Earth.

3. The Clouds Are The Place Where He Unites to His People

The clouds also symbolize the realm of the Spirit where we become one in Jesus. Another Hebrew word for cloud is

"**Chishshur**", which means **"unite"** and is also the "**hub of a wheel**" where its spokes unite.[21]

The word "*Chishshur*" conveys the idea of the Spirit of the Lord uniting His Body unto Himself.

While Jesus was on Earth no one could be His Body, but as He manifests Himself in the clouds, He gathers all of us inside of Him to form part of His spiritual Body.

> *And if I go and prepare a place for you, I will come again and receive you unto Myself, that where I am, there ye may be also. And whither I go ye know, and the way ye know.*
>
> *John 14:3-4*

In the Book of Ezekiel, we see how the Spirit of the living creatures moved inside the wheels, in the "*Chishshur*" of God. It's in the "*Chishshur*" where the Spirit of God who gives life and unifies is found.

> *Wherever the spirit wanted to go, they went, because there the spirit went; and the wheels were lifted together with them, for the spirit of the living creatures was in the wheels.*
>
> *Ezekiel 1:20*

> *And the glory which Thou gavest Me I have given them, that they may be one, even as We are one: I in them and Thou in Me, that they may be made perfect in one, and that the world may know that Thou hast*

---

[21] 2840. rÚ˝vIj chishshur, khish-shoor´; from an unused root meaning to bind together; combined, i.e. the nave or hub of a wheel (as holding the spokes together):—spoke.

sent Me and hast loved them, as Thou hast loved Me. "Father, I will that they also, whom Thou hast given Me, **be with Me where I am, that they may behold My glory which Thou hast given Me;** for Thou loved Me before the foundation of the world

John 17:22-24

Jesus sat on His throne and shared His Glory with us. We are not separated from the Lord waiting to go join Him up in the clouds.

If He lives in us and we live in Him, we are already eternally united. Where He is, there we also are. He came in the Spirit so we would be ONE with The Father and with Him. We are no longer separated from Him.

5. Clouds represent People

Jesus comes in the midst of the clouds to judge those who do evil.

> *These are wells without water, clouds that are carried by a tempest, for whom the mist of darkness is reserved forever.*
>
> 2 Peter 2:17

> *These are spots on your feasts of charity when they feast with you, feeding themselves without fear. Clouds they are without water, carried about by winds; trees whose fruit withereth, without fruit, twice dead, plucked up by the roots;*
>
> Jude 1:12

6. Clouds Represent Times of Judgment

*That day is a day of wrath, a day of trouble and distress, a day of waste and desolation, a day of darkness and gloominess, a **day of clouds** and thick darkness,*
Zephaniah 1:15

*Behold, he shall come up as **clouds**, and his chariots shall be as a whirlwind. His horses are swifter than eagles! Woe unto us, for we are despoiled!*
Jeremiah 4:13

*a day of darkness and of gloominess, **a day of clouds** and of thick darkness, as the morning spread upon the mountains. A great people and a strong, there hath not been ever the like; neither shall be any more after it, even to the years of many generations.*
Joel 2:2

This prophecy is fulfilled when Jesus takes The Throne and He gives His Authority and the Kingdom to the saints of the Most High.

7. Every Eye Shall See Him

Behold, He cometh with clouds, and every eye shall see Him, and they also who pierced Him; and all kindreds of the earth shall wail because of Him. Even so. Amen.
Revelation 1:7

We see here that in His coming *"every eye shall see Him"*.

Now, Jesus told His disciples that He would come in a form the world could not see Him but they would.

> *Yet a little while and the world seeth Me no more, but ye see Me. Because I live, ye shall live also.*
>
> John 14:19

The words "*every eye shall see Him*" was a Jewish expression that meant something was a fact. It was the same as saying, "*it will be evident*" or "*it shall be commonly known*". We see this same expression in the *Book of Isaiah* when he prophesied about the Glory of God that would come when *John the Baptist* was to submerge Jesus in the Jordan.

> *The voice of him that crieth in the wilderness: "Prepare ye the way of the LORD; make straight in the desert a highway for our God.*
>
> *Every valley shall be exalted, and every mountain and hill shall be made low; and the crooked shall be made straight, and the rough places plain.*
>
> *And the glory of the LORD shall be revealed, and **all flesh shall see it together**; for the mouth of the LORD hath spoken it."*
>
> Isaiah 40:3-5

When Jesus was baptized, the Heavens opened and everybody who was there heard the Father acknowledge the Son:

> *...and the Holy Ghost descended in a bodily shape like a dove upon Him, and a voice came from Heaven, which said, "THOU ART MY BELOVED SON; IN THEE I AM WELL PLEASED."*
>
> Luke 3:22

This was not broadcasted via satellite to all the nations, however it says all flesh jointly saw Him. The disciples and the followers of Jesus recognized that Glory, but not the religious folk and those who crucified Him.

Peter talks about another similar moment when they saw the Glory of Jehovah during Jesus' transfiguration.

> *For we have not followed cunningly devised fables when we made known unto you the power and coming of our Lord Jesus Christ, but **were eyewitnesses of His majesty.** For He received from God the Father honor and glory when there came such a voice to Him from the Excellent Glory: "This is My beloved Son, in whom I am well pleased." And this voice, which came from Heaven, we heard when we were with Him on the holy mount.*
>
> 2 Peter 1:16-18

When Christ manifests Himself among His people, those who are His disciples see Him. He is *The one Who was, Who is and Who is come*, and *is constantly coming* (**erchomai**) The Almighty, and there are ongoing testimonies of His manifestation through visions of all sorts and appearances which occur in the midst of a prophetic realm.

How many times do we say: "*The Lord is entering the midst of the congregation at this moment*," or "*we see Him extending His hand and doing miracles?*" How many times during warfare manifestations do we not see Him coming on His white horse and His angels with Him? How many times have we not seen His Arm extended and His brightly shining sword bringing Righteousness over a city, or been immersed in an intense cloud of His Presence?

If this is not happening to you, it's because you are either not amidst a prophetic atmosphere or you don't believe this can happen to you.

The reality is that there are thousands and thousands who have experienced manifestations of this type.

14 RECEIVING THE LORD IN THE CLOUDS

When we speak about subjects, such as this, I believe that no one has the last word and it is not my desire to impose anything on anyone, but to give light to see a different perspective.

My intention is to analyze this subject from a prophetic perspective and from the fundamental principles we have been studying and to bring some light that I am sure will bless you.

> *For the Lord Himself shall descend from Heaven with a shout, with the voice of the archangel and with the trumpet of God; and the dead in Christ shall rise first; then we who are alive and remain shall be caught up together with them in the clouds to meet the Lord in the air. And so shall we ever be with the Lord. Therefore comfort one another with these words.*
>
> *1 Thessalonians 4:16-18*

I want to first subdivide this subject so it will be easier to understand what the Apostle Paul was trying to bring across.

1. We Are Already In and With The Lord

Before attempting to interpret this theme, we have to part from the fact that the heart of The Gospel is that those of us, who already belong to Him, are already eternally united to Him.

A P O C A L Y P S E   The Revelation of Jesus Christ

In Him we live, we move and have our being.
Acts 17:28

In Him we have access to heavenly places, and if He allows us, we can even be caught up in Heaven or be present in front of His Throne.

Paul himself, in that same letter to the *Thessalonians* tells us how we are already united to Him.

For God hath not appointed us to wrath, but to obtain salvation by our Lord Jesus Christ who died for us, that, whether we wake or sleep, **we should live together with Him.**
1 Thessalonians 5:9-10

The interpretation of this passage where we are snatched away to receive the Lord in the clouds, then this has to mean something different than a future union with Jesus. **This way of seeing things suggests that we are not completed in Him nor Him in us.**

In all of his epistles, Paul emphasizes the power that this represents, to be united with Christ. One example is:

But he that is joined unto the Lord is one spirit.

1 Corinthians 6:17

Paul never suggests that this union is partial or incomplete. Remember what the Apostle Peter said about the writtings of the Apostle Paul, and this is where many twist his teaching, since they are hard to understand.

I believe it speaks about a personal entering into His presence; a powerful encounter with Jesus in which He genuinely joins His Spirit with ours. In my case, I have had that type of experience many times. The one at the island of *Patmos* was one of them.

2. What does it mean to be snatched away?

His cloud is real and to be snatched into it, transforms us from Glory to Glory. Not every person that calls Him "*Lord, Lord*" has this type of experience, only those who have died to their flesh to love Him and follow Him.

The word "*clouds*" in this Scripture is "***nephele***" in Greek[22] and means *cloudiness*. This is the same word used to determine the cloud of witnesses in *Hebrews Chapter 12*.

Paul was talking to the *Thessalonians* regarding the destiny of those who had died in Christ and were already part of the cloud of witness and of the Eternal Body of Christ; and also about the instant transformation of those who were still alive as they were wrapped in His cloud of Glory.

Let's remember they were living in times of great tribulation waiting for the Righteousness of God to manifest over their enemy, the *Roman Empire*.

The brethren asked each other what happened to those who died in Christ before He would manifest Himself? (Referring to the judgment they were awaiting and that would come in the year 70 A.D.)

---

[22] 3507. nefe÷lh nephele, nef-el'-ay; from 3509; properly, cloudiness, i.e. (concretely) a cloud: — cloud.

I believe, and what's been revealed to me, is that this scripture refers to Jesus coming to dwell within us. Jesus in His **Chishshur** *(cloud - navel of a wheel)* joins for Himself His eternal Body and makes us ONE with Him and with the Father. This is in agreement with the word "to catch up" in the epistle to the Thessalonians which comes from the word "*harpazo*" that means *to grab, hold*[23] and that derives from the word "*haireomai*" that also means to take for oneself.

Jesus told His disciples that He would come again to take us unto Himself so we could always be with Him *(John 14:1-2)*. He said He was going to come back to us to make His dwelling place within us. At the moment He comes to our heart, we are transformed thoroughly and we are able to hear His voice and to experience His Presence inside His Cloud of Glory. It's when we genuinely are born of the water and of the Spirit that we become like the wind, like the air where He then meets us to direct us by His Spirit *(John 3:6-8)*.

3. The Cloud of His Presence

The cloud of His Presence, in this case is the word **nephele**, which is the same used to describe the cloud of witnesses. The nephele is the presence of the Lord manifested in a cloud that unites in an instant the believers from every time period, those that were before Christ and those who were alive at that time. This cloud is constantly growing as more and more people join the Lord as they depart from this world.

---

[23] *726. aJrpa¿zw harpazo, har-pad'-zo; from a derivative of 138; to seize (in various applications): — catch (away, up), pluck, pull, take (by force).*

138. aiJre÷omai, hahee-reh'-om-ahee;. probably akin to 142; to take for oneself, i.e. to prefer: — choose. Some of the forms are borrowed from a cognate e°llomai hellomai which is otherwise obsolete.

It was the same "*baptism in the cloud*" Israel experienced at the time of Moses and which Paul speaks about to the Church.

> *Moreover, brethren, I would not have ye ignorant of how all of our fathers were under the cloud, and all passed through the sea, and all were **baptized unto Moses in the cloud** and in the sea. And all ate the same spiritual meat, and all drank the same spiritual drink; for they drank of that spiritual Rock that followed them, and that Rock was Christ.*
>
> 1 Corinthians 10:1-4

> *For the cloud of the LORD was upon the tabernacle by day and fire was on it by night, in the sight of all the house of Israel throughout all their journeys.*
>
> Exodus 40:38

This cloud is a type and shadow of the Glory of God that rests over the Kingdom believer who is now the Tabernacle of God on Earth.

4. Resurrected In our Spirits

At the sound of His voice, when the revelation of Christ manifests in our lives, we become conscious that we are one single Eternal Body who goes to unite with Him from generation to generation.

In Christ, we are already resurrected in His Kingdom by His Glory to live with the Lord forever and this is what transforms our entire being. Paul knew this and taught it:

> *If ye then be risen with Christ, seek those things which are above, where Christ sitteth at the right hand of God. Set your affection on things above, not on things on the earth.*
> *For ye are dead, and your life is hid with Christ in God. When Christ, who is our life, shall appear, (**Phaneroo**- manifest[24]), then shall ye also appear with Him in glory.*
> *Colossians 3:1-4*

If our life is hidden in Christ and we are jointly resurrected with Him then that transformation manifests in our lives. His voice resounds in us like an explosion of resurrection life that continuously quickens us.

This is consistent with what Isaiah said regarding Christ living in us:

> *Arise, shine, for thy light is come, and the glory of the LORD is risen upon thee. For behold, the darkness shall cover the earth and gross darkness the people; but the LORD shall arise upon thee, and His glory shall be seen upon thee. And the Gentiles shall come to thy light, and kings to the brightness of thy rising.*
> *Isaiah 60:1-3*

Now going back the passage of *1st Thessalonians 4:17* we see it is intimately related to *1st Corinthians 15* where Paul describes to them the resurrection in a spiritual body of those who are in Jesus.

---

[24] 5319. fanero/w phaneroo, fan-er-o'-o; from 5318; to render apparent (literally or figuratively): — appear, manifestly declare, (make) manifest (forth), shew (self).

> *It is sown a natural body; it **is raised a spiritual body**. There is a natural body, and there is a spiritual body. And so it is written: "The first man Adam was made a living soul." The last Adam was made **a quickening Spirit**.*
>
> *However that which is spiritual was not first, but that which is natural, and afterward that which is spiritual. The first man is of the earth, earthy; the second Man is the Lord from Heaven. As is the earthy, such are they also that are earthy; and **as is the heavenly, such are they also that are heavenly**.*
>
> *And as we have borne the image of the earthy, we shall **also bear the image of the heavenly**. Now this I say, brethren, that **flesh and blood cannot inherit the Kingdom of God**; neither doth corruption inherit incorruption. Behold, I show you a mystery: We shall not all sleep; but we shall all be changed in a moment, in the twinkling of an eye, at the last trumpet. For the trumpet shall sound, and the dead shall be raised incorruptible, and we shall be changed.*
>
> 1 Corinthians 15:44-52

Let's note that the passage of *Thessalonians 4:16-17* is exactly the same as the last part of these verses in *1 Corinthians 15:*

> *For the Lord Himself will descend from heaven with a shout, with the voice of an archangel, and with the trumpet of God. And the dead in Christ will rise first.*

> *Then we who are alive and remain shall be caught up together with them in the clouds to meet the Lord in the air. And thus we shall always be with the Lord.*
>
> *Thessalonians 4:16-17*

Although Paul is certainly talking about the ultimate resurrection of the dead, he is also establishing a principle regarding the transformation undergone by those who are alive and whose spirit have been resurrected in Christ Jesus.

> *If ye then be risen with Christ, seek those things which are above, where Christ sitteth at the right hand of God*
>
> *Colossians 3:1*

The Church is the image of Christ. In Him we carry The Image of the Heavenly One. Resurrection starts to manifest in our lives, as we are still alive, quickening our mortal bodies.

Now let's go back to the explanation Paul is giving about transformation when we resurrect in Christ.

5. The Resurrection is Our Heavenly Habitation

> *For this corruptible must put on incorruption, and this mortal must put on immortality. So when this corruptible* **shall have put on incorruption**, *and* **this mortal shall have put on immortality**, *then shall be brought to pass the saying that is written:* **"Death is swallowed up in victory."**
>
> *1 Corinthians 15:53-54*

We see in this scripture two things we need to put on: *incorruption* and *immortality*.

Paul is talking about being genuinely clothed in our heavenly dwelling, which is Christ. Resurrection begins in those who have died in Christ, those who have crucified their desires and passions, while they are still alive in this world.

In his second epistle to the *Corinthians,* Paul again addresses the topic of being clothed in our heavenly dwelling and how to achieve it.

> *For we know that if our earthly house, this tabernacle, were dissolved, we have a building of God, a house not made with hands, eternal in the heavens.*
> *For in this we groan, earnestly desiring to be clothed about with our house which is from Heaven, that,* **being so clothed, we shall not be found naked***.*
> *For we that are in this tabernacle do groan, being burdened, not because we would be unclothed, but clothed about,* **that mortality might be swallowed up by life***.*
> 2 Corinthians 5:1-4

Paul talks about being found clothed by our heavenly house so all that is mortal could be swallowed up by life. If he says "*we shall be found clothed*" clearly indicates that he is not referring to something that happens after death, but while we are still alive.

Jesus promised to return spiritually to be our habitation, to make us dwell with Him, to be our resurrection while we're still in this body from now and evermore.

We will not die even though we will leave our earthly bodies behind. We will not go to sleep as it happened to the saints of the Old Covenant. At the moment of parting this world, we will instantaneously be in His Presence completely alive; we will only be divested of our flesh.

> *O death, where is thy sting? O grave, where is thy victory?" The sting of death is sin, and the strength of sin is the law. But thanks be to God,* **who giveth us the victory** *through our Lord Jesus Christ!*
> *1 Corinthians 15:55-57*

This verse is key for us to realize that Paul talks about the effectiveness of the resurrection dwelling in us.

> *And concerning the dead, that they rise: have ye not read in the book of Moses, how in the bush God spoke unto him, saying, `I am the God of Abraham, and the God of Isaac, and the God of Jacob'? He is not the God of the dead, but the God of the living. Ye therefore do greatly err."*
> *Mark 12:26-27*

We can see through his writings that Paul was determined to reach the state of resurrection while he was still alive.

That is why he urges us to groan to be clothed by our house in heaven, that mortality might be swallowed up of life.

The same concept he wrote to the Philippians:

And be found in him, not having mine own righteousness, which is of the law, but that which is through the faith of Christ, the righteousness which is of God by faith:

*That I may know him, **and the power of his resurrection**, and the fellowship of his sufferings, being made conformable unto his death;*

*If by any means **I might attain unto the resurrection** of the dead.*

***Not as though I had already attained**, either were already perfect: but I follow after, if that I may apprehend that for which also I am apprehended of Christ Jesus.*

*Brethren, **I count not myself to have apprehended**: but this one thing I do, forgetting those things which are behind, and reaching forth unto those things which are before,*

I press toward the mark for the prize of the high calling of God in Christ Jesus.

Philippians 3:9-14

In this Scripture it is obvious that he is trying to reach out for the resurrection while he is alive. That is why he says: "***I count not myself to have apprehended.***" This clearly indicates that he is not referring to the final resurrection of the dead, but to something that is attainable while we are in this world. He emphasizes that he is reaching forth to apprehend that for which he was also apprehended of Christ Jesus.

The transformation of all of our being spirit, soul, and body is a constant that we see throughout his epistles. This is why I think and is my understanding that this verse in Thessalonians Chapter 4 has a much deeper and different meaning that the traditional interpretation, of a rapture.

6. His Manifestation In Our Midst

Jesus also talked about how the manifestation of His Presence (parousia) would be. He was talking to those who would enter great persecution in their time. He needed to encourage them in the face of the approaching tribulation.

> *I will not leave you comfortless; **I will come to you**. Yet a little while and the world seeth Me no more, but **ye see Me**. Because I live, ye shall live also.*
>
> *At that day ye shall know that I am in My Father, and you in Me, and I in you. He that hath My commandments and keepeth them, he it is that loveth Me; and he that loveth Me shall be loved by My Father, and I will love him and **will manifest Myself to him**."*
>
> *Judas (not Iscariot) said unto Him, "Lord, how is it that **Thou wilt manifest Thyself unto us**, and not unto the world?"*
>
> *Jesus answered and said unto him, "If a man loves Me, he will keep My words; and My Father will love him, and **We will come unto him and make Our abode with him**.*
>
> John 14:18-23

We see here once again how the covering of His Tabernacle is the key to His manifestation. He returned to them and He did not leave them comfortless. They saw Him because He made His abode with them as He does with us.

This coming back to indwell those who love Him is obviously not the second coming.

According to what we have been studying, *"Jesus Coming in the Clouds"* has to do with His manifestation as King of Kings governing and ruling Earth with the believers. This implies that this transformation happens when His voice, which sounds like a trumpet, reveals in us the glorified Christ who quickens our spirit. Trumpets are symbols of the prophetic voice. In an instant our dormant spirit is brought to life to see and hear The Kingdom of God.

I was in the Spirit on the Lord's Day, and I heard behind me a great voice as of a trumpet, saying, "I am Alpha and Omega, the First and the Last," and, "What thou seest, write in a book and send it unto the seven churches which are in Asia:

Revelation 1:10 & 11a

John heard the trumpet and gives us the example of how the revelation of His Glory progresses in the life of a believer opening up for him/her the heavenly dimensions.

The apostles heard Jesus, while He was speaking about His return, that some of them would be alive at that moment and will see His day.

And he said unto them, Verily I say unto you, That there be some of them that stand here, which shall not taste of death, till they have seen the kingdom of God come with power.

Mark 9:1

This was fulfilled when the Apostle John, as well as others, were still alive when Jesus manifested the power of His Kingdom in the destruction of Jerusalem in 70 A.D. After that, the Power of His Kingdom manifests in all sort of blessings as well as in judgements, and He gives this power to rule with Him to whosoever believes in Him.

15 HEAVEN'S SUPREME COURT

> *And Jesus said unto them, "Verily I say unto you, that ye that have followed Me, in the regeneration when the Son of Man shall sit on the throne of His glory, ye also shall sit upon twelve thrones, judging the twelve tribes of Israel.*
>
> *Matthew 19:28*

As we have seen throughout this book, Jesus grants the saints the faculty to judge. He opened the way so as His saints, we can boldly enter before the Throne and once inside, watch how Heaven is organized to release Judgment. It is the man-child of the **Book of Revelation** Chapter 12 who has access to Heaven to judge with the rod of iron.

> *And she brought forth a man-child, who was to rule all nations with a rod of iron: and her child was caught up unto God, and to His throne.*
>
> *Revelation 12:5*

This *man-child* represents the overcoming believers who have denied their life unto death; the ones who learned to wrestle against the devil and subject him under their feet. There are always words of triumph in their mouth to remind satan of all the ways they have defeated him. These are the words of their testimony.

APOCALYPSE The Revelation of Jesus Christ

And they overcame him by the blood of the Lamb and by the word of their testimony, and they did not love their lives to the death.

Revelation 12:11

1. The Supreme Court in Heaven: The 24 Elders

Once we overcome in every commandment found in the seven letters Jesus gave to the churches in *Asia*, we are then ready to be promoted to understand the **Supreme Court of Heaven** and its Judgments. Overcoming establishes our position and opens the doors of Heaven for us.

The Apostle John, a first fruit of that overcoming Church, is raptured into Heaven (like many are nowadays) to see and be part of God's amazing Government-design prepared for His Church.

Note that John was at one level "*in the spirit*" (in Chapter One) and then in chapter 4 he enters into a higher and deeper level of this experience. He moves from the level of "Revelation" into the level of "Government."

> ***I was in the Spirit*** *on the Lord's Day, and heard behind me a great voice, as of a trumpet...*
>
> *Revelation 1:10*

> *After this I looked, and, behold, a door was opened in Heaven: and the first voice which I heard was as it were of a trumpet talking with me; which said, Come up hither, and I will shew thee things which must be hereafter.*

Dr. Ana Méndez Ferrell

And immediately I was in the spirit*: and, behold, a throne was set in Heaven, and One sat on the throne.*

Revelation 4:1-2

Revelation is granted through intimacy and the pursuit of God, but rulership comes only by overcoming the system of *Babylon*. There is a type of authority granted unto us by Grace as part of our redemption, however there is another one that is conquered. In The Kingdom of God, Heaven and Earth operate jointly.

Around the Throne in Heaven, there are 24 Elders and 4 Cherubim or Living Creatures. Twenty-four is the number of perfect government, it's the divine design Jesus gave His Church to govern and judge: she is part of His Supreme Court of Justice

And He that sat was to look upon like a jasper and a sardius stone: and there was a rainbow round about the throne, in sight like unto an emerald.
*And round about the throne were **four and twenty seats**: and upon the seats I **saw four and twenty elders** sitting, clothed in white raiment; and they had on their heads crowns of gold.*

Revelation 4:4

This is the model Jesus left us to be a victorious, Heavenly-directed, living organism; the Church built-up by Him, whom the gates of hell cannot prevail against.

The Elders are called by this name since they manifest the character of God. We see in the book of *Daniel* The Father called by a term having the same meaning: *Ancient*. His Throne is Fire since this is the element that symbolizes His judgments.

APOCALYPSE The Revelation of Jesus Christ

I beheld till the thrones were cast down, and the Ancient of Days sat down, whose garment was white as snow and the hair of His head like the pure wool. His throne was like the fiery flame, and His wheels as burning fire.

A fiery stream issued and came forth from before Him. Thousand ministered unto Him, and ten thousand times ten thousand stood before Him: the judgment was set, and the books were opened.

Daniel 7: 9-10

...until the Ancient of Days came, and judgment was given to the saints of the Most High; and the time came that the saints possessed the Kingdom.

Daniel 7:22

And I saw thrones and they that sat upon them, and judgment was given unto them.

Revelation 20:4

These twenty-four Elders are not people John could recognize. They are certainly not the twelve tribes of *Israel* and they are neither the twelve apostles as individuals but as a representation of the Church government. John is not seeing himself or his fellow Apostles upon any of the Elder's thrones.

This number is symbolic and represents the divine structure of Government in every nation and in every city of the world.

And they sung a new song, saying, Thou art worthy to take the book, and to open the seals thereof: for thou wast slain, and **hast redeemed us to God by thy**

Dr. Ana Méndez Ferrell

blood out of every kindred, and tongue, and people, and nation;
And hast made us unto our God kings and priests: and we shall reign on the earth.

Revelation 5:9-10

Understanding the place of *"Elders"* is key in The Kingdom of God. Today, when we talk about Elders in the Church we think of them as the group of leaders under a senior Pastor, but this was never intended to be this way.

Elders are the key component to bring The Kingdom of God into the Earth. As Paul established churches during his traveling, he assigned *"elders"* over the cities and not *"pastors"* over congregations.

For this cause left I thee in Crete, that thou shouldest set in order the things that are wanting, and ordain **elders** *in every city, as I had appointed thee:*

Titus 1:5

Elders have a burden and a comprehension about their city and also about their God-given authority to rule over it alongside other elders. They don't think in terms of "my congregation" or "my network" but in terms of God's Kingdom being established in every area of society within the city and how they are the ones responsible to make it happen as a team.

God has to reposition men and women into the right places where He has called them to minister. The whole structure of the Church has to be lined up with His designs and not with those we have inherited from *Babylon* in the XVI century. For this to happen, He has already started a major reformation of Heavenly and prophetic understanding so we can rule and reign with Him under His terms and not under ours.

This is not about destroying churches and pastors, He is *reforming them* into a new understanding so we can all walk as ONE Church in the Victory and the Power He has given us.

Many of those functioning as *Apostles*, *Prophets* and *Pastors* will be repositioned by God to function within His system of Justice.

2. God Wants Elders In The World Today

As we can see in this Heavenly design, first of all, Elders are overcomers over *Babylon*. They have been promoted to constantly be around the Throne. They understand true worship and that's what keeps them in this very close position to God. They move deeply in the prophetic dimension of Heaven to grab hold of what Heaven is saying at all times. It is from this understanding and knowledge of Heaven that they can properly rule over the earth.

They have entered a level of God's glory only granted to those who have been able to understand God's judgments and the way He establishes His justice. In this level we see four living creatures, which are the very Cherubs that move and operate within the glory of God; it's the Glory of His Righteousness that judges everything that opposes Him.

> *And before the throne there was a sea of glass like unto crystal: and in the midst of the throne, and round about the throne, were four beasts full of eyes before and behind. And the first beast was like a lion, and the second beast like a calf, and the third beast had a face as a man, and the fourth beast was like a flying*

eagle. And the four beasts had each of them six wings about him; and they were full of eyes within: and they rest not day and night, saying, Holy, holy, holy, Lord God Almighty, Who was, and is, and is to come.
Revelation 4:6-8

They are full of eyes because they see every circumstance from every possible angle in order to judge according to God's wisdom.

The Elders are in agreement with the four living creatures who let them know *how* to judge and rule from Heaven down to Earth.

Each one of these Cherubs has been given to understand a different perspective of God's judgments. *The Lion* sees from the point of view of God - The King; *the calf*, from the eyes of Jesus' servant hood; *the man*, from His overcoming humanity; and *the eagle* from the manifold wisdom of an uprisen, lifted-up Spirit, the very perspective of Heaven.

A biblical case of this manner of judging is how God dealt with His servant *Paul of Tarsus*. On one end he was a murderer, but on the other end he had the zeal of God and with great boldness he endeavored on what he erroneously deemed was God's Will. God did not judge him solely for the wrongness; instead He saw what was favorable in his character and transformed him into a great apostle.

Both the Living Creatures and the Elders are constantly acknowledging the Headship, the sovereignty and the Glory of God. They always aim to exalt God's achievements, never man's.

The Elders display their authentic humility by casting down their crowns so the exaltation only goes to the Lord and not to men.

What is important for them is their position around the Throne, and not that their names are known. They are not pursuing fame or to have the largest crowd or the biggest church, although they may have it. They never want to loose their place and their Heavenly function. They are not in competition with one another but in agreement and fellowship because they all hear the same things coming from the Throne. They spend time together so they can all experience and hear the instructions from God in order to be accurate in their judgments and counsel.

The Throne of God can be seen from many characteristics and many angles. In the case of Chapters 4 and 5 from the **Book of Revelation,** the ones being manifested are *righteousness* and *judgment.* The 24 Elders are immersed in the midst of God's powerful Presence that produces thunder and lightning similar to what Moses saw in *Mount Sinai,* as he was approaching the terrible Presence of God to receive the Law. The mount was smoking and thunder and fire were surrounding its summit. He was receiving the authority to rule, to counsel and to release the judgments of God. Moses was face to face with God's Glory, the same manner we see the twenty-four Elders before the Throne.

> *And out of the throne proceeded lightnings and thunderings and voices: and there were seven lamps of fire burning before the throne, which are the seven Spirits of God.*
>
> *Revelation 4:5*

The seven spirits are in the midst of them because the Elders rule with the understanding of the fullness of the Spirit.

In Chapter 5 of the **Book of Revelation** we see the One on the Throne holding a scroll that none in Heaven or Earth could open and John is saddened because of this. We clearly see here the operation of Heaven before the first coming of Christ and after His ascension. Before Messiah came, no one could release God's judgments. It's the Elders who are around the Glory, those who see Jesus as King in His full authority, the ones who are able to bring this revelation to the Body of Christ represented by John here.

> *And one of the elders saith unto me, Weep not: behold, the Lion of the tribe of Judah, the Root of David, hath prevailed to open the book, and to loose the seven seals thereof. And I beheld, and, lo, in the midst of the throne and of the four beasts, and in the midst of the elders, stood a Lamb as it had been slain, having seven horns and seven eyes, which are the seven Spirits of God sent forth into all the earth.*
>
> *Revelation 5:5-6*

The Elders have the power to release the Authority of the *Lion of Judah* and a deep revelation of the Cross from Heaven that will execute The Judgments of the Lamb.

Until the Elders reveal this aspect of Messiah, then the Church (John) is able to see the Lamb upon the Throne next to The Father. This is not just talking about the Lamb being enthroned as everybody does but instead, in having a true knowledge of this fact in our innermost being.

> **And I beheld, and, lo, in the midst of the throne** *and of the four beasts, and in the midst of the elders, stood a Lamb as it had been slain...*
>
> *Revelation 5:6a*

APOCALYPSE The Revelation of Jesus Christ

John is beholding the transition between God's government in the Old Testament- The Father seated at His Throne- and Jesus in His Kingdom seated at the Throne with His Father which includes the saints, through the structure of Eldership of the New Covenant.

Notice the difference between Chapter 1 and Chapter 5 in the ***Book of Revelation***. In the first one, representing the Old Government, the Father is upon The Throne and the seven Spirits are before Him. In the New, (Chapter 5) The Father and the Lamb are merged on the Throne and the seven spirits are **within** Jesus.

Elders see the Lamb beyond the bounds of Salvation as the One now sitting on the Throne and possessing the full manifestation of the Holy Spirit. This is the core of their message and the way they manifest God's presence to the Church.

They see and point us to Jesus so we can see Him in all His Power and in all the manifold Wisdom and Knowledge of the true baptism of the Spirit.

The Church needs the rising up of the Elders who see Jesus on His throne and can say *BEHOLD!* ...opening up the eyes of the believers to see Him as He really is in His glory and Authority.

Another important characteristic of Elders is their passion to worship God.

> *And when He had taken the book, the four living beings and the four and twenty elders fell down before the Lamb, having every one of them harps and golden vials full of incense, which are the prayers of saints.*
>
> *Revelation 5:8*

The Heavenly harps given to the Elders are the revelation of prophetic worship. They understand the sounds of Heaven and the new songs in order to bring them down to the earth.

Elders bring the atmosphere of God into a place through their worship. This type of adoration is directed by the Holy Spirit and has nothing to do with our beautifully written songs; it's a new song. As they bring the realm of Heaven down, the prayers of the saints are activated before the Throne.

There is a close relationship between the harps and the vials of incense.

It is not the function of the Elders to pray for the needs of the body making the people dependent on them, lazy and ignorant. Instead they teach the people how to pray and through their worship and position before the Throne they add power to their prayers. I don't mean by this that they do not pray for the people, of course they do; everyone than knows the heart of the Father intercedes for His beloved. We see this same effect in Chapter 8.

> *And another angel came and stood at the altar, having a golden censer; and there was given unto him much incense, that he should offer it with the prayers of all saints upon the golden altar, which was before the throne.*
>
> *And the smoke of the incense, which came with the prayers of the saints, ascended up before God out of the angel's hand.*
>
> *And the angel took the censer, and filled it with fire from the altar, and cast it onto the earth; and there were voices and thunderings and lightnings, and an earthquake.*
>
> *Revelation 8:3-5*

Elders are also assigned by God to bring forth the revelation of the Heavenly reality to the believers. They exercise an apostolic ability to make Heaven real and to establish the promises of God among His people.

> *Then, addressing me, one of the elders [of the Heavenly Sanhedrin] said, Who are these [people] clothed in the long white robes? And from where have they come?*
>
> *I replied, Sir, you know. And he said to me, These are they who have come out of the great tribulation (persecution), and have washed their robes and made them white in the blood of the Lamb.*
>
> *For this reason they are [now] before the [very] throne of God and serve Him day and night in His sanctuary (temple); and He Who is sitting upon the throne will protect and spread His tabernacle over and shelter them with His presence.*
>
> *They shall hunger no more, neither thirst any more; neither shall the sun smite them, nor any ascorching heat.*
>
> *For the Lamb Who is in the midst of the throne will be their Shepherd, and He will guide them to the springs of the waters of life; and God will wipe away every tear from their eyes.*
>
> *Revelation 7:13-17 Amplified*

As I previously stated, the saints referred to in this chapter are not those who are already dead but those who are still alive on Earth. That is why He shepherds them and leads them to the living waters. In Heaven they don't need protection, nor are they in a desert needing water.

The Elders reveal to the Church (John) the position and the power of those who overcome their trials. Because Elders live worshipping before the Throne they can bring words from Heaven to encourage the believers. They don't feed the people but make sure that the Lamb feeds them and quenches their thirst. They lead the Church to serve before the Throne and not to serve around a man.

3. The Church receives the Faculty to Judge

Besides the Elders, the angels and the archangels appear before the Throne to carry out the sentences of the Most High and convey them to the Saints so they decree them and come to pass.

> *"This matter is by the decree of the watchers, and* ***the demand by the word of the holy ones****, with the intent that the living may know that the Most High ruleth in the kingdom of men, and giveth it to whomsoever He will, and setteth up over it the basest of men."*
> *Daniel 4:17*

> *...until the Ancient of Days came, and* ***judgment was given to the saints of the Most High;*** *and the time came that the saints possessed the Kingdom.*
> *Daniel 7:22*

> *... saying, "Hurt not the earth, neither the sea nor the trees,* ***till we have sealed the servants of our God in their foreheads."***
> *Revelation 7:3*

Who are these chosen ones? These are the ones who are with Him and follow Him wherever He goes.

"These shall make war with the Lamb, and the Lamb shall overcome them; for He is Lord of lords and King of kings, and they that are with Him are called, and are chosen, and faithful."

Revelation 17:14

The number of the Chosen is symbolic and is 144.000. This is a prophetic number that symbolizes all the saints from every time period. 12 represent the Kingdom. 12 x 12 = 144 is the manifested Kingdom or God's Supreme Government. 1,000 symbolizes the countless, hundreds of thousands, or *"its number is like the stars in the Heaven or the sand of the sea."*

Therefore sprang there even of one, and him as good as dead, so many as the stars of the sky in multitude, and as the sand which is by the sea shore innumerable.

Hebrews 11:12

And they sang, as it were, a new song before the throne, and before the four living beings and the elders; and no man could learn that song, except the hundred and forty and four thousand who were redeemed from the earth.

These are they that were not defiled with women, for they are virgins. These are they that follow the Lamb whithersoever He goeth. These were redeemed from among men, being the firstfruits unto God and to the Lamb.

Dr. Ana Méndez Ferrell

> *And in their mouth was found no guile, for they are without fault before the throne of God*
>
> *Revelation 14:3-5*

Some examples of *the number 1000* in the Bible are:

> *And the women answered one another as they played, and said, "Saul hath slain his thousands, and David his ten thousands."*
>
> *1 Samuel 18:7*

1,000 also symbolizes that which is perfect = 10 x 10 x 10, meaning Heaven itself.

> *Then I looked, and I heard the voices of many angels on every side of the throne and of the living creatures and the elders [of the Heavenly Sanhedrin], and they numbered ten thousand times ten thousand and thousands of thousands,*
>
> *Revelation 5:11 Amplified*

> *After this I looked and a vast host appeared* **which no one could count**, *[gathered out] of every nation, from all tribes and peoples and languages. These stood before the throne and before the Lamb; they were attired in white robes, with palm branches in their hands*
>
> *Revelation 7:9 Amplified*

The Chosen ones are in continuous contact with the prophetic and worship according to Heavens' worship, which is why they have a new song. They have washed their garments in the Blood of the Lamb and are the true Tabernacle of God on Earth. The dwelling place of God is above every tribulation: those who dwell herein have laid hold of everything Jesus has conquered at the cross of Calvary and drink from the living waters of the Lamb.

16 GOD'S JUDGMENTS

The LORD reigneth, let the earth rejoice! Let the multitude of isles be glad thereof! Clouds and darkness are round about Him; righteousness and judgment are the habitation of His throne.

A fire goeth before Him, and burneth up His enemies round about. His lightnings enlightened the world; the earth saw and trembled.

The hills melted like wax at the presence of the LORD, at the presence of the Lord of the whole earth.

The Heavens declare His righteousness, and all the people see His glory.

Psalm 97:1-6

Along with the previous Chapter, this is our last basic *Key Theme of Interpretation* to know God as *Supreme Judge of the Universe*.

Although the Earth has been under the power of darkness, the ONLY Sovereign God has always been Jehovah. The devil is not an authority nor does he understand government, these are attributes only God has and those whomsoever He gives them to.

He has reigned throughout the centuries executing Righteousness and Judgment over all the nations. He is slow to anger and abounding in mercy but on the day He acts, His judgments are manifested.

APOCALYPSE The Revelation of Jesus Christ

The Day Of The LORD

God's time is different than ours.

> *But, beloved, be not ignorant of this one thing: that with the Lord one day is as a thousand years, and a thousand years as one day.*
>
> 2 Peter 3:8

In general, the interpretation given when we hear the expression *"The Lord's Day"* or *"the Day of the Vengeance of our God"* has been as the *"End of All Things"*.

On one hand, futurist theologians associated this "*day*" with *"The Great Tribulation"* in which the seals, the trumpets and the vials of the Apocalypses (*Book of Revelation*) are poured out over a latter generation, which is the one receiving the accumulated wrath of God. This would make God an unjust Judge. Why would one single generation have to pay for the atrocities the world has committed throughout centuries? On the other hand, the total, final *"End of the World"* as we know it, is also attributed to this day.

The reality is that it has nothing to do with a particular day, or with one period or with two periods, instead it symbolizes *each* time period when Jehovah has released and will release His wrath.

Allow me to explain this thoroughly. The first thing we need to understand is that there was an imminent judgment that Jesus predicted over Old Covenant *Israel* and over the *Jerusalem* of His time. As we saw before, there is a clear division in Scripture between the Ancient World or Era, and the New.

Dr. Ana Méndez Ferrell

> *"The Spirit of the Lord GOD is upon Me, because the LORD hath anointed Me.... To proclaim the acceptable year of the LORD, and **the day of vengeance of our God;***
>
> *Isaiah 61:1a & 2a*

In this passage Isaiah uses the word '*year*' to determine a period of grace for the preaching of the Gospel IN ISRAEL. Until the day of His ascension, the ministry of Jesus was solely to the Jews. It was His People He warned about how one day He would return (spiritually) to judge *Israel* thereby destroying the Temple and the ancient priestly and sacrificial system.

With the crucifixion, the cup of wrath was filled to the brim. *Jerusalem* had been the city that killed all the prophets of God and finally ended the life of the Messiah.

Jesus' death, unleashes a time period referred to as *"The Wrath of God"* on the Heavenly clock. By His Grace The Father granted a time of patience so The Gospel could be preached and a large amount of the people from that generation could be saved. In the scripture we just read Isaiah calls that time period the '*Acceptable Year of the Lord'*.

> *The Lord is not slack concerning his promise, as some men count slackness;* ***but is longsuffering*** *to us-ward, not willing that any should perish, but that all should come to repentance.*
>
> *2 Peter 3:9*

That patience necessarily had to be referring to the generation living at the time since it is possible to increase the number of believers in one generation and for less people to be lost; this is not true in the sum total of generations.

If we extend this period of patience to countless number of generations century after century, the margin of lost souls will be increasing since more people are born in the world than those who are saved in each generation.

Let's think using this small mathematical formula: every 40 years, symbol of a generation, millions of people go to hell. There are nations at this precise moment that have less than 1% of Christianity. Despite the stunning growth of the Gospel during these last decades we are not even 5% of the world population.

If Jesus' longsuffering refers to waiting throughout the centuries for less people to become lost, the Christian population nowadays would have to be 90% of humanity, then the wait would be worth it. On the contrary, history shows the Earth has lived practically in darkness from the Second Century to date.

If the Day of the Lord announced by the prophets and the apostles was soon to happen in our days, God would lose the battle since the devil would take the majority of humanity to hell.

Jesus was talking about the Judgment coming over the generation of His days; to love them and prepare them He sent His Holy Spirit so everyone could have the opportunity to be saved.

In Chapters 2 and 3 of *Joel*, the Lord talks about the impressive manifestation of His Grace sent before the Judgment of the years 66 to 70 A.D.

> *And it shall come to pass afterward, that I will pour out my spirit upon all flesh; and your sons and your daughters shall prophesy, your old men shall dream dreams, your young men shall see visions:*

And also upon the servants and upon the handmaids in those days will I pour out my spirit.

And I will shew wonders in the heavens and in the earth, blood, and fire, and pillars of smoke.

The sun shall be turned into darkness, and the moon into blood, before the great and terrible day of the LORD come.

Joel 2:28-31

"The End" was prophecied to come after the outpouring of the Holy Spirit, not 2000 plus years after.

There are many other passages that also refer to the Messiah's Grace being poured throughout *Israel* mentioned as brooks and streams of water revitalizing the dry land.

And upon every high mountain and upon every high hill there will be brooks and streams of water in the day of the great slaughter [the day of the Lord], when the towers fall [and all His enemies are destroyed].

Isaiah 30:25 Amplified

The "*Fall of the Towers*" is narrated in the "Wars of the Jews." This happened during the siege of Jerusalem and its destruction in the year 70 A.D.

The believers were able to escape to the mountains as Jesus instructed them, thus saving their lives during the siege.

Even though the Holy Spirit and God's grace manifested greatly before the judgment, of course, He is available to every person throughout generations and His grace towards us never ends nor do His wells of Living Water ever end.

2. The Language of God Concerning His Judgments

God's expressions and manner of speech many times differ from ours. For example, when God uses expressions such as "the Heavens shall roll up as a scroll, "the stars shall fall from their place," "the sun and the moon shall shine no more," or "the Earth shall forever be desolate and never again shall the son of man inhabit it," we think about the end of the world, but God here is only referring to a judgment, of course, one of great magnitude.

We see this clearly when the prophets Isaiah, Jeremiah, Ezekiel, Amos and Obadiah prophesy *Edom*'s total destruction. If we interpret it literally it appears that Jehovah will erase it from the map. However nowadays that land corresponds to the beautiful land of Jordan with godly churches on it. *(Jeremiah.49:33, Book of Revelation 6:13-14, Isaiah 34:2-4 y 8-10)*

We see the same expressions of total destruction on the "*Day of the Lord's Wrath*" when Isaiah predicts judgment over ancient *Babylon*. This prophecy was fulfilled when the Medes and the Persians conquered it.

> ***Behold, the day of the LORD cometh, cruel, both with wrath and fierce anger, to lay the land desolate; and He shall destroy the sinners thereof out of it. For the stars of Heaven and the constellations thereof shall not give their light; the sun shall be darkened in his going forth, and the moon shall not cause her light to shine.*** *And I will punish the world for their evil and the wicked for their iniquity; and I will cause the arrogance of the proud to cease, and will lay low the haughtiness of the terrible. I will make a man more precious than fine gold, even a man than the golden wedge of Ophir.*

> *Therefore **I will shake the Heavens, and the earth shall remove out of her place,** in the wrath of the LORD of hosts and in the day of His fierce anger.*
>
> *"Behold, I will stir up **the Medes** against them, who shall not regard silver; and as for gold, they shall not delight in it.*
>
> Isaiah 13: 9-13, 17

The Earth was not destroyed neither was it removed from its place yet *Babylon* was conquered by the Medes and Persians; the second Heaven was shaken and the *Babylon*ian system of those days was crushed down. Malachi also prophesies like Isaiah regarding the *Coming of the Lord* as a *"Day of Judgment"*, not to destroy His people, but to refine them.

> *"**But who may abide the day of His coming**? And who shall stand when He appeareth? For **He is like a refiner's fire** and like fullers' soap. And He shall sit as a refiner and purifier of silver; and He shall purify the sons of Levi, and purge them as gold and silver, that they may offer unto the LORD an offering in righteousness."*
>
> Malachi 3:2-3

This is a prophecy that anounces the Lord's coming to polish Israel before their great judgement.

God, in His Greatness and Righteousness will not pour out the full burning of His wrath over one single last generation - that would be unjust. The generation of our time is full of abominations and is undoubtedly attracting God's judgments upon themselves, however each generation and every nation have also felt them.

3. The Judgments of *The Book of Revelation*

If we understand that God is Righteous for every era and for every kindred, then we will realize that the **Book of Revelation** is the Revelation of Jesus as a governing Judge. To govern is to Judge and to establish Righteousness.

The judgments and the plagues in this book are centered against a spiritual government called *Babylon*. This is the evil's empire main structure as we studied before.

In a spiritual sense, *Babylon* was established over the *Jerusalem* of Jesus' time. The whole religious system had been corrupted and was reaching its end. Its sins resembled *Egypt*'s and its spiritual fornication equaled Sodom's.

> *And their dead bodies shall lie in the street of the great city, which spiritually is called* ***Sodom and Egypt, where also our Lord was crucified.***
> *Revelation 11:8*

> *And the woman whom thou sawest is that great city which reigneth over the kings of the earth."*
> *Revelation 17:18*

Jesus appeared to John initially to declare to him the Judgment coming over *Jerusalem* and over the spiritual *Babylon*ian empire that had overtaken her.

In all these passages where we see the seals, the woes, the trumpets and the vials, they have to do first of all, with the judgment over the Old System and the fall of the old *Jerusalem*; thereafter with the revelation of God's Judgments throughout all time periods.

He displays Himself to John as the One Who is; Who was, and the One who comes (***erchomai-*** verb in *Aoristo* tense, not related to any time frame).

A group of Roman emperors subdued *Israel* in an unprecedented tribulation. *Jerusalem* was besieged and destroyed in the year 70 A.D. and those who were able to flee to the mountains, saved their lives. ***(I write about this historic recount in Appendix /Instrument # 2)***

4. Judgments Throughout History

> *And I saw, and behold a white horse: and he that sat on him had a bow; and a crown was given unto him: and he went forth conquering, and to conquer.*
>
> *And there went out another horse that was red: and power was given to him that sat thereon to take peace from the earth, and that they should kill one another: and there was given unto him a great sword.*
>
> *And when he had opened the third seal, I heard the third beast say, Come and see. And I beheld, and lo a black horse; and he that sat on him had a pair of balances in his hand.*
>
> *And I looked, and behold a pale horse: and his name that sat on him was Death, and Hell followed with him.*
>
> *And power was given unto them over the fourth part of the earth, to kill with sword, and with hunger, and with death, and with the beasts of the earth.*
>
> *Revelation 6:2, 4,5,8*

God's Judgments have been released through the ages. I believe the white horse represents the believers that have received the faculty to judge: the overcomers that are coming out to establish God's Judgments over the Earth. The red horse, symbol of *death and war*, has been released many times throughout history, likewise the black one that represents *shortages and famine* and the pale one that releases *sickness and plagues*

Earthquakes, tsunamis, hurricanes, tornadoes, merciless fires, hail, financial crisis are all forms of how God judges the nations; sometimes it's to bring conviction of sin and repentance; and others, it's to severely punish due to the iniquity and the arrogance of men.

Other Judgments include the *terrible plagues* and *epidemics* that have scourged humanity. During the pests of the Middle Ages people cried out wanting to die because of the pain and the brokenness from this disease. A third of the world population died in 1918 during the Spanish Influenza. *AIDS* is a clear judgment of God against sexual aberrations.

The amount of dead people, congenital malformations and organ destruction caused by vaccines and the side effects of pharmaceutical science is yet another form of Judgment.

I personally had a vision about the **Book of Revelation** *Chapter 9* where I saw millions of demons come out from the abyss with syringes (stings) in their hands and infringe substances upon people which would damage their organs with great pain. Spiritually they wore golden crowns, which are the exaltation of the scientific mind, and their faces were like men, they appeared humanitarian but were murderers. They made much noise with their lying advertisements on TV and through every media source making people addicted to medication they never required or that would heal them either.[25] They had breastplates; they were

---

[25] *I recommend my book Pharmakeia, Health's Assassin, so you understand this subject in depth. .*

protected by governments and the insurance companies. Their end is not to heal but to destroy because its leader is Apollyon, the destroyer. And I saw how God judged those who put their trust in science and not on Him.[25] *(See footnote)*

Another way of judgment is through *unrighteous* and *stern governments*. God has allowed *tyrant kings* and *dictators* to subdue the peoples. In the Old Covenant He turned *Israel* over to be enslaved by *Egypt* then by *Babylon* and then persecuted by *Assyria*. He also allowed *unjust judges* and *wicked kings* to govern over it to teach them repentance and faithfulness to Him.

In the Christian era we have seen these same tyrants full of wickedness such as Hitler, Mussolini, Stalin, Saddam Hussein, Fidel Castro and others. These are persons dominated by an unrelenting thirst to dominate the world, ruled by satan himself to kill and destroy and govern by terrible oppression.

The seal, the trumpets, the vials of the ***Book of Revelation*** are diverse manners God judges the Earth, not as one major event but repeatedly throughout history.

5. Angels Interact with The Church to Bring Forth The Judgments of God

We see all throughout the ***Book of Revelation*** the existing relationship between the angels and John. They reveal things to him, they transfer him from one place to another in the Heavenly dimensions and in the regions where the great powers of darkness live and act.

In *Chapter 10* we see an angel giving John a little book to eat and after doing so, he is given the mandate to prophesy to every tongue and nation.

> *And I took the little book out of the angel's hand and ate it up, and it was in my mouth sweet as honey; and as soon as I had eaten it, my belly was bitter.*
> *And he said unto me, "Thou must prophesy again before many peoples and nations, and tongues and kings."*
>
> *Revelation 10:10-11*

Historically this never happened, there is no evidence that John ever traveled everywhere taking a message. This therefore speaks to us either as a symbol of the Church receiving the prophetic word and taking it to every nation, or as John's spirit, in the same manner Elijah's spirit did, is manifested bringing us the mysteries of God.

The Spirit of Prophecy is determinant in understanding the dimensions of the Spirit. It's within this realm where the Church is being trained to rule and understand how and when to loose a judgment that has come from the Throne of God.

I want to make it clear that the Judgments of God cannot be released by just any immature Christian; but by the Elders, the Apostles and Prophets that form the system of Justice of The Kingdom of God.

6. Judgments Prompt the Battles of Heaven

Every spiritual battle we fight on earth has a Judgment at its core. During these, we see how an army of angels fights alongside the Church. Many times Michael is the one heading an important battle.

They fight in the invisible spheres but God gives us the title of "*battle overcomers*".

> *And there was war in Heaven: Michael and his angels fought against the dragon; and the dragon fought and his angels, And they (the saints) overcame him by the blood of the Lamb and by the word of their testimony, and they loved not their lives unto the death.*
>
> *Revelation 12:7, 11*

> *I have commanded My sanctified ones; I have also called My mighty ones for Mine anger, even them that rejoice in My highness." They come from a far country, from the end of Heaven, even the LORD and the weapons of His indignation, to destroy the whole land.*
>
> *Isaiah 13:3.5*

7. Diverse Angels In The Book of Revelation

Angels are our fellow servants and work with us in many forms. They are our servants when they operate under our authority and they are co-servants when they have a parallel work they have to accomplish along and with us. The angel that was speaking to John was a co-servant.

During our missions on Earth there are co-servant angels that accomplish a lot of the spiritual work for our ministries. They do the heavenly part and we do the earthly one.

When somebody receives the authority from God to legislate from Heaven and to fight next to The Lamb, all these angels will be at their disposition.

We see in the **Book of Revelation** diverse types of angelical messengers. Learning about them helps us to pray and loose them according to the leading of the Spirit.

Getting to know angels is a two-edged weapon. There have been many cases in history where immature Christians received angelical visitations and ended up worshipping them or depending on them more than from God, facing sudden destruction afterwards.

Some may ask: "Why do we need angels, if we have the Holy Spirit operating through us?"

Angels are like voltage regulators of the Glory of God. Some messages, should we receive them directly from the realm of God's Glory, will simply scorch us. The Apostle John was undoubtedly Spirit-filled, however he received the message of the **Book of Revelation** through the angel of Jesus Christ.

Judgment Angels

They are in charge of opening the seals, the vials, the trumpets, the earthquakes, the plagues and other forms of judgment and have done this throughout history.

Angels of the 4 Winds

These are in charge of everything that has to do with winds. They can either loose them or stop them. In this next scripture they are restraining them, but this is not their only assignment in eternity.

> *And after these things I saw four angels standing on the four corners of the earth, holding the four winds of the earth, that the wind should not blow on the earth, nor on the sea, nor on any tree.*
> *Revelation 7:1*

The Angel of the Eternal Gospel

This is an angel that has been active throughout the ages. We see him operating in the Old Testament as it's mentioned in *Hebrews 4:2,* and we can also release him to bring revival to our cities.

> *And I saw another angel fly in the midst of Heaven, having the everlasting **gospel** to preach unto them that dwell on the earth, and to every nation, and kindred, and tongue, and people.*
> *Revelation 14:6*

> *For unto us was the gospel preached, as well as unto them: but the word preached did not profit them, not being mixed with faith in them that heard it.*
> *Hebrews 4:2*

The Angel of Incense

> *And another angel came and stood at the altar, having a golden censer; and there was given unto him much incense, that he should offer it with the prayers of all saints upon the golden altar, which was before the throne.*
> *Revelation 8:3*

APOCALYPSE The Revelation of Jesus Christ

Angels of Glory

And after these things, I saw another angel come down from Heaven, having great power; and the earth was lightened by his glory.

Revelation 18:1

Angels that carry out prophetic acts from Heaven

Then a mighty angel took up a stone like a great millstone, and cast it into the sea, saying, "Thus with violence shall that great city Babylon be thrown down, and shall be found no more at all.

Revelation 18:21

Messenger Angels that perform prophetic acts from Heaven

Then a mighty angel took up a stone like a great millstone and threw it into the sea, saying, "Thus with violence the great city Babylon shall be thrown down, and shall not be found anymore.

Revelation 18:21

Jailer Angels - God's Police

And I saw an angel come down from Heaven, having the key to the bottomless pit and a great chain in his hand.

And he laid hold on the dragon, that serpent of old, who is the devil and satan, and bound him for a thousand years.

Revelation 20:1-2

These angels are also the ones that help us chain the spirits of sorcerers and witches that come in their astral bodies to attack the body of Christ, they are powerful enough to put them in chains and arrest the major powers and principalities.

Executing Angels

These are the angels that execute the judgments of God over cities and nations bringing forth the Lord's justice over wickedness; the wine press of the Earth has been treaded many times.

> *And another angel came out of the Temple, which is in Heaven, he also having a sharp sickle.*
> *And another angel came out from the altar, who had power over fire, and cried with a loud cry to him that had the sharp sickle, saying, "Thrust in thy sharp sickle and gather the clusters of the vine of the earth, for her grapes are fully ripe."*
> *Revelation 14:17-18*

Angels to the Churches

These are the angels that help and minister to the church in each city. These type of angels are very useful because they bring forth strategies from Heaven for the Church and reveal God's thoughts regarding the way we are building.

> *The mystery of the seven stars which thou sawest in My right hand, and the seven golden candlesticks: the seven stars are the angels of the seven churches, and the seven candlesticks which thou sawest are the seven churches.*
> *Revelation 1:20*

SECTION 3

THE BOOK OF REVELATION'S SECONDARY SUBJECTS

17 THE GREAT TRIBULATION

In the previous section we saw how the people of *Israel* were living in a time of great tribulation, which culminated in God's great judgment upon *Jerusalem*. The Temple was destroyed and the city set ablaze.

The Apostle John writes his prophetic message and lets them know God has not abandoned them but instead He is about to manifest His Righteousness in an extraordinary manner.

He begins the **Book of Revelation** by letting them know that he himself is part of the tribulation.

> *I, John, who also am your brother and companion in the **tribulation** and in the Kingdom and patience of Jesus Christ, was on the isle that is called Patmos, for the Word of God and for the testimony of Jesus Christ.*
>
> *Revelation 1:9*

In the **Book of Revelation** Chapter 7, he mentions a tribulation; due to its context it leads me to believe that he is referring to the Church of all times. If indeed the primitive Church lived in an unprecedented tribulation, we also need to overcome our own tribulations to serve God effectively.

APOCALYPSE The Revelation of Jesus Christ

This chapter talks about the manifestation of The Kingdom of God in the midst of our tribulations, whether personal or collectively.

Let's remember that we are studying the **Book of Revelation** as the Living Government of Christ with His saints.

And one of the elders answered, saying unto me, "Who are these that are arrayed in white robes, and from whence have they come?"

*And I said unto him, "Sir, thou knowest." And he said to me, "These are they that came out **of great tribulation**[26], and have washed their robes and made them white in the blood of the Lamb.*

Revelation 7:13-14

For this reason they are [now] before the [very] throne of God and serve Him day and night in His sanctuary (temple); *and He Who is sitting upon the throne will protect and spread His tabernacle over and shelter them with His presence.*
They shall hunger no more, neither thirst any more; neither shall the sun smite them, nor any scorching heat.
For the Lamb Who is in the midst of the throne will be their Shepherd, and He will guide them to the springs of the waters of life; and God will wipe away every tear from their eyes.

Revelation 7:15-17 Amplified Bible

This passage has traditionally been interpreted as a "future great tribulation," a sort of a third world war where millions of people die and are brought before the Throne of God.

---

[26] *Many manuscripts do not include the word "great", only using: "these are they that came out of tribulation."*

First of all is important to notice that these people **"Come out" of great tribulation**, this means they did not die but came out of it. So from verse 15th on, we see a parallel to ***Book of Revelation*** Chapter 21 which is the manifestation of *God's Tabernacle over the Earth* and The Kingdom of God established by the Messiah.

Be reminded that we first studied the *Basic Themes of Interpretation*, which shed light for us to interpret the secondary ones, or the ones derived from these.

The fact that the Lamb shepherds those in white garments and leads them to fountains of water makes it clear to us that they are not in Heaven but on Earth where the spiritual waters of Christ are needed. In Heaven there are no dry places and nobody needs to be led to the fountains of water —which are the life of Jesus — they are already eternally immersed in Him.

These points set the standard for our interpretation since throughout the centuries God's Tabernacle with men is the Church of Jesus Christ on Earth. God's Tabernacle will not be established after a future world war, it has already been established in the midst of His people. We are the Temple of God and His throne is in the midst of His Church and we therefore serve Him continually.

The way I see this passage, John is talking about the victorious Church; those who overcome their own individual tribulations and the standards set by Jesus in the letters to the seven churches of *Asia*. It refers to those who have washed their clothes in the Blood of the Lamb and serve God in the understanding of His throne and His Kingdom. They have become true kings and priests unto God ministering from His Tabernacle where God's Presence continually comes (*erchomai*) to His people.

The Spirit of God continually manifests as a Cloud of Glory in our midst and Jesus is revealed to us from glory to glory. **We are continually being baptized in the Holy Spirit, which is the Cloud that carries His Presence.**

Throughout centuries, in every tongue and nation there is an invisible barrier that has to be crossed: these are the tribulations that bind us to this world until Jesus is formed in us and then we will rule and reign with Him. Those who allow themselves to be led by the Spirit are the ones who are before the Throne aligned with what the Lord wants to say and do.

> *...strengthening the souls of the disciples, exhorting them to continue in the faith, and saying, "We must go through many tribulations to enter the kingdom of God."*
>
> Acts 14:22

> *If we endure we shall also reign with Him.*
>
> 2 Timothy 2:12a

When we endure suffering of any kind, it is for the purpose of The Kingdom of God to manifest in our lives. As we understand this, something powerful forms within us.

The Kingdom of God, and His Throne begin to convey the answers to us and we see Victory over that particular tribulation. This overcoming power emerges from within us positioning us in a new level of authority and government over that area of our lives.

When we see Victory over our tribulations, we are taken to the Springs of Life in Christ, and His Tabernacle grows within us.

Dr. Ana Méndez Ferrell

When I suffer, I learn to reign!

My little children, over whom I travail in birth again until Christ be formed in you.
Galatians 4:19

As we talk about God's judgments in the course of this study, we will see that He has sent many tribulations of great devastation to humanity applicable to Jesus' prophecies.

To think that the Lord needs to bring a devastating destruction over the Earth so His kingdom would be established it is not a thought that lines up with the mind of Christ.

Certainly, there are strong shakings coming to the Earth, because the Lord needs to judge evil and men's abominations that are now overwhelming the world. The very Earth can not take any longer the sin of humanity and is vomiting iniquity through natural disasters. Yet God will make us who fear Him come out triumphant from any tribulation.

18 THE BEAST

To address this subject, it is necessary to look at many points of view. As a Prophetess of God, this is what the Lord has revealed to me and I am sure other revelations over that can converge with this one to attain a full meaning.

In a literal sense, *"the Beast"* in the **Book of Revelation 13** refers to the *Roman Empire*. I believe this is due to Daniel's interpretation of Nebuchadnezzar's dream. He saw an enormous image composed of four kingdoms whose feet represented *Rome*. *(Daniel 2:34-35)*

This image is the full composition of the *Babylonian* system or *"The Great Harlot"* whose final defeat comes when Jesus overcomes it at the Cross and then sends His judgment over *Rome*. (In my book *"The End of an Era"* I enter into great detail about this subject.)

*And the stone that smote the image **became a great mountain and filled the whole earth..***

*And in the days of these kings shall the God of Heaven set up a Kingdom which shall never be destroyed; and the Kingdom shall not be left to other people, but it shall break in pieces and consume **all these kingdoms**, and it shall stand for ever.*
Daniel 2:35b, 44

We see clearly how The **Kingdom of the Messiah** is the great **Mount Zion** that was established over the whole Earth. ALL THOSE KINGDOMS WERE DESTROYED by the Rock that is Jesus. *Rome* was literally burned down several times after God's judgment was decreed over it.

On the eve of July 19th, 64 A.D., a fire began in *Rome* that lasted 9 days. Ten of the fourteen districts disappeared and along with them the Temple of Jupiter. History attributes this catastrophe to Emperor Nero.

Regardless, this was not the only time *Rome* was burnt down -*"the beast received a mortal wound but survived"*- another great fire takes place in 69 A.D. during the empire of Vitellius and a third fire destroys it in the year 80 under the government of Emperor Titus.

The beasts in the Bible are symbols of empires controlled by dominions of darkness, **not of individuals**.

The ***Book of Revelation*** doesn't mention "*an antichrist*" but "*a beast*". John is the only apostle who uses the word "antichrist" and he does it in relation to a spirit that was moving among them already. He knew what he was talking about since he is the one who received the ***Book of Revelation***.

However, every generation has to defeat the spirit of the antichrist.

> *Little children, it is the last time: and as ye have heard that antichrist shall come, even now are there many antichrists; whereby we know that it is the last time*
>
> *1 John 2:18*

> *Who is a liar but he that denieth that Jesus is the Christ? He is antichrist that denieth the Father and the Son.*
> *1 John 2:22*

> *For many deceivers are entered into the world, who confess not that Jesus Christ is come in the flesh. This is a deceiver and an anti-christ.*
> *2 John 1:7*

The apostate Israel, during the time of Jesus, carried in them the spirit of the anti-christ. What John is saying is that everyone that denies that Jesus is the Messiah, is the anti-christ.

Now then, the beast is an empire, and the anti-christ is a spirit, that was already among them and still is in the world today. These are two different things.

"*The Beast*" is the demonic spirit behind every *Babylon*ic system throughout history. It's the spirit of humanism that gives rise to the ideology of a superman rising as God; it's the fallen man ruled by the *Tree of Good and Evil*; it's Cain's homicidal seed that grows from generation to generation promoting lawlessness on Earth and opposing the True God.

> *Beloved, believe not every spirit, but test the spirits whether they are of God, because many false prophets have gone out into the world.*

> *Hereby know ye the Spirit of God: Every spirit that confesseth that Jesus Christ is come in the flesh, is of God.*

APOCALYPSE The Revelation of Jesus Christ

*And every spirit that confesseth not that Jesus Christ is come in the flesh, is not of God; and such is **the spirit of Antichrist**, whereof ye have heard that it should come, and **even now already it is in the world**.*

*Ye are of God, little children, and **have overcome them**, because greater is He that is in you than he that is in the world.*

They are of the world; therefore they speak of the world, and the world heareth them.

1 John 4:1-5

If it was already in the world in the time of John the Apostle, it is very clear that is not something we have to expect to show up in the future.

1. The Mark of The Beast

In a literal sense, it referred to the allegiance that some Jews made with Rome in order to save their lives during the time of the siege in the year 70. The siege of Jerusalem lasted many months, and only those who sold themselves to the Romans were allowed to leave outside the walls. Nobody could sell or buy anything. Since there was nothing left, and they were dying by the thousands, the hunger got to such extreme that they entered into cannibalism. Two pounds of wheat were sold for a talent, as well as six pounds of barley.

In a broad sense, whenever the Lord speaks about marking men in the Bible, in all the other cases it has always been a spiritual mark. Cain is marked to be protected when he was cursed to be a fugitive and vagabond in the world and this mark was spiritual.

When we see the angels marking the chosen ones, they don't put a tatoo or a microchip in their forheads, but a seal of light that is visible in the spiritual realm.

The same thing happens when we talk about the mark of the beast. This is visible as a seal of darkness that God and even the demons can clearly see.

Being marked by the beast is when someone's mind (in the forehead) and actions (right hand) are controlled by the systems of this world in full corruption. Being marked is being totally sold out to darkness, unchanging, a lover of darkness more than light.

> *For men shall be lovers of their own selves, covetous, boasters, proud, blasphemers, disobedient to parents, unthankful, unholy,*
> *Without natural affection, trucebreakers, false accusers, incontinent, fierce, despisers of those that are good, Traitors, heady, highminded, lovers of pleasures more than lovers of God;*
> 2 Timothy 3:2-4

> *Now as Jannes and Jambres withstood Moses, so do these also resist the truth:* **men of corrupt minds, reprobate concerning the faith**.
> 2 Timothy 3:8

The "*right hand*" also speaks about authority and the power of our own will to make decisions.

My husband has a powerful revelation on the subject of "*the mark of the beast*". He saw Cain being marked because of his sin of murder. This mark is the mindset of the serpent, which is the beast in the *Garden of Eden* and entered him as the result of the fall. This is not the mark God gave him to protect him, but the one satan implanted in his soul. This mark passed on as a seed through the generations carrying the unrepentant attitude of Cain.

It is from Cain's seed that the entire *commercial system* developed that is under the control of the king of Tyrus, *god of trade and commerce* and under Mammon the god of riches. He is the first one ever mentioned in the Bible to build a city, which was the first form of society. This was the first city satan ruled and then perfected it as the ancient city of *Babylon*.

> *And Cain knew his wife; and she conceived, and bare Enoch:* **and he builded a city***, and called the name of the city, after the name of his son, Enoch.*
> *And unto Enoch was born Irad: and Irad begat Mehujael: and Mehujael begat Methusael: and Methusael begat Lamech.*
> *And Lamech took unto him two wives: the name of the one was Adah, and the name of the other Zillah.*
> *And Adah bare Jabal: he was the father of such as dwell in tents, and of such* **as have cattle.**
> *And his brother's name was Jubal: he was the father of all such* **as handle the harp and organ.**
> *And Zillah, she also bare Tubalcain, an instructer of* **every artificer in brass and iron:** *and the sister of Tubalcain was Naamah.*
>
> *Genesis 4:17-22*

Let's remember that the great *Babylon* is the city that rules over all the kings of the Earth, and that she controls the economical world system. When John is watching her judgment in Heaven, he tells about the merchant's great sorrow as they saw her burning in fire.

And the woman which thou sawest is that great city, which reigneth over the kings of the earth.

...

The merchants of these things, which were made rich by her, shall stand afar off for the fear of her torment, weeping and wailing,

...

And the voice of harpers, and musicians, and of pipers, and trumpeters, shall be heard no more at all in thee; and no craftsman, of whatsoever craft he be, shall be found any more in thee; and the sound of a millstone shall be heard no more at all in thee;

Revelation 17:18; 18:15 & 22

There is a form of commerce that is righteous based on the principles of God, which is a blessing to many and differs totally from the evil one where *Babylon* controls people through greed, and by abusing others to get gain.

Being marked by "the beast" is having the mark of evil, the mark of Cain. These are the kind of people *Jude* talks about in His epistle.

For there are certain men crept in unawares, who were before of old ordained to this condemnation, ungodly men, turning the grace of our God into lasciviousness, and denying the only Lord God, and our Lord Jesus Christ.

Jude 4

Woe unto them! for they have gone **in the way of Cain***, and ran greedily after the error of Balaam for reward, and perished in the gainsaying of Core.*

> *These are spots in your feasts of charity, when they feast with you, feeding themselves without fear: clouds they are without water, carried about of winds; trees whose fruit withereth, without fruit, twice dead, plucked up by the roots;*
> *Raging waves of the sea, foaming out their own shame; wandering stars, to whom is reserved the blackness of darkness for ever.*
> *And **Enoch** also, the seventh from Adam, prophesied of these, saying, Behold, the Lord cometh with ten thousands of his saints,*
> *To execute judgment upon all, and to convince all that are ungodly among them of all their ungodly deeds which they have ungodly committed, and of all their hard speeches which ungodly sinners have spoken against him.*
> *These are murmurers, complainers, walking after their own lusts; and their mouth speaketh great swelling words, having men's persons in admiration because of advantage.*
>
> Jude 11-16

Six is *the number of man.* The code of the beast is *666* which is the number of man that exalts himself over God; the superman that is god in himself and that worships satan in all his disguised forms such as money, lust, and all kinds of perversion.

Today we see this kind of thinking in the "*New Age*" and in books such as "*The Secret*". We see the abominable abuse of corrupted men controlling the stock market and the financial destiny of nations. Sexual deprivation, greed and crime are getting to intolerable climaxes.

The *666* is not a microchip, neither a credit card, nor a tatoo. It is the spiritual mark of the evil men that oppose God.

Men like Hitler, Mussolini, the Illuminati and others have identified themselves with this number, as one that carries magicals powers to conquer the world.

19. THE TIMES IN THE BOOK OF REVELATION AND THE RESURRECTION OF THE DEAD

1. The Times in the *Book of Revelation*

From the beginning of our study, we saw how the dimensions of God are not limited by time in accordance to the Earth. The clock of men does not run Heaven. God is Eternal and there is no time in Him.

He is *The One Who Was, Who Is, and Who Comes* or *is continually coming* (**erchomai**). He is the Great "I Am", *the Eternal Present* Who manifests Himself within the temporality of man. For this reason a heavenly book such as the **Book of Revelation** cannot be interpreted with the times of Earth.

In Chapter 10 when John is about to eat the small book of prophecy, we see the angel telling John that time *ceased to be.*

> *And he swore by Him that liveth for ever and ever, who created heaven and the things that are therein, and the earth and the things that are therein, and the sea and the things which are therein, that **there should be time no longer,** but that in the days of the voice of the seventh angel, when he shall begin to sound, **the mystery of God should be finished, as He hath declared to His servants the prophets.***
>
> *Revelation 10:6 & 7*

The mystery of God is consummated when Jesus takes The Throne sitting at the right hand of The Majesty on High. From here onward, His Kingdom has no end.

The true Church enters The Kingdom and into the timeless dimensions of God from where He governs. The little book the angel gives John is *the Government Manual for the prophetic dimensions of The Kingdom*. If we understand this timeless nature of Heaven, it makes it easy for us to interpret some of the passages such as *"the thousand years"*.

A. The Thousand Years of the *Book of Revelation*

> *And I saw an angel come down from Heaven, having the key to the bottomless pit and a great chain in his hand.*
>
> *And he laid hold on the dragon, that serpent of old, who is the devil and satan, and bound him for a thousand years.*
>
> *And he cast him into the bottomless pit, and shut him up and set a seal upon him, that he should deceive the nations no more till the thousand years should be fulfilled; and after that he must be loosed a little season.*
>
> *Revelation 20:1-3*

It's important to understand this expression *"the thousand years"* from its Hebrew etymology, which is **Atid Lavo**. This literally means *"the coming age"* and is also used as a term that means *"The Messianic Age"*.

In other words, as we enter the prophetic dimension, which is the Messiah's Kingdom, we enter into the timelessness of His Kingdom.

"*A thousand*" as we previously saw, speaks to us about that which is perfect: 10 x 10, this is Heaven, God's Spiritual Kingdom.

"*We will reign one thousand years*" means we will rule from the spiritual world. The Kingdom of Christ on Earth is eternal; it doesn't end in a limited period of a thousand years.

> *Of the increase of His government and peace there shall be no end, upon the throne of David and upon His Kingdom, to order it and to establish it with judgment and with justice from henceforth even forever. The zeal of the LORD of hosts will perform this.*
>
> *Isaiah 9:7*

We see this as well in the expression used by *Peter*:

> *But, beloved, be not ignorant of this one thing: that with the Lord one day is as a thousand years, and a thousand years as one day.*
>
> *2 Peter 3:8*

The fact that Peter makes the comparison between *a day* and *a thousand years* clearly makes us understand that it's not dealing with a precise time period. Among the Hebrews, *the day of YHWH* carries the understanding of "*a coming future*" or "*the beginning of the Messianic age*".[27]

---

[27] Same as footnote Number 23 on page 190.

Jesus said, quoting *Isaiah 61*, that He had come to proclaim *"the acceptable year of The Lord"*, that had to do with the period of grace that preceded *"The day of Vengeance of our God"* that was coming soon.

This year, that the Lord spoke about, was not one consisting of 365 days, since actually it lasted 37 years. Neither did the Day of vengeance last 24 hours, this judgment lasted three and a half years of great tribulation, and another three and a half years after the destruction of Jerusalem and the Temple.

We also see the number one thousand in *Psalm 105*:

> *He hath remembered his covenant for ever, the word which he commanded to* **a thousand generations.**
> *Psalm 105:8*

The meaning of this Psalm is not that after a thousand generations, He forgets about His covenant, instead it says it is forever.

B. satan bound and then loosed

> *And when the thousand years are expired, satan shall be loosed out of his prison, and shall go out to deceive the nations to the four quarters of the earth -- Gog and Magog -- to gather them together for battle, the number of whom is as the sand of the sea.*
> *Revelation 20:7-8*

We clearly understand this passage when we learn to live in the dimensions of The Kingdom of God, when we genuinely stop being of this world to depend on a Kingdom whose laws and physics are very different than the Earthly ones.

The devil has been bound for us; he can never penetrate The Kingdom of God to bring us harm.

Furthermore, to live in this spiritual reality is a continuous victory. The enemy has been thrown out of heaven's access he once had and now lives among the nations of the Earth, deceiving them. It's outside The Kingdom where he is loose and where the battle is at, and millions of people, Christians included, are living the devils' onslaught because of not having entered the dimensions of the Spirit of God.

Now, even though we have entered The Kingdom of God and we live within the *Eternal Reality* (thousand years) it's by going through trials and tribulations that we mature in Christ. God allows satan to interfere in our lives for our own growth.

The expression *"satan will be loosed to deceive the nations"* has to do with these trials we have to overcome even if we are kings and priests. He is loose for a short time in our daily walk to fulfill this purpose.

Messiah's Kingdom is eternal, that's how it was prophesied to be. Nowhere in the Old Testamentarian concept was it written that the reign of the Messiah would be for a limited time of *"a thousand years"*. In Jesus, Heaven and Earth are joined together and this truth applies for both dimensions.

> *And I will make her lame a remnant, and her that was cast far off a strong nation; and the LORD shall reign over them in Mount Zion **from hence forth, even for ever.***
>
> *Micah 4:7*

> *And He will reign over the **house of Jacob** throughout the ages; and of His reign there will be no end.*
>
> *Luke 1:33*

In the *Hebraic Gematria*[28] the expression "Gog or Magog" (*Gog and Magog)* form the number 70. The Jewish sages interpret this as the 70 Gentile nations, which represent the world. Nevertheless the Bible doesn't say that God is going to gather the nations for the battle but only *Gog* and *Magog*. We know this because in Greek, the pronoun "*them*" is in the masculine case as opposed to "*nations*" that is a neutral noun.

> *And when the thousand years are expired, satan shall be loosed out of his prison, and shall go out to deceive the nations to the four quarters of the earth -- Gog and Magog -- to gather **them** together for battle, the number of whom is as the sand of the sea.*
>
> *Revelation 20:7-8*

If we paraphrase this Bible passage, it would say something like this:

"Outside the dimensions of God's Kingdom (1000 years) the devil, out of his prison, carries on deceiving the nations, but God will combat these spirits."

---

[28] *Among the Hebrews there is a science named Gematria through which every letter of the alphabet has a number and these in turn carry a symbolism worthy to interpret.*

CONCLUSION

Many are the themes found in the **Book of Revelation** and it would take me various volumes to go into greater detail in each one. Some are quite profound and require of us to first digest what I mention in this book. **The Kingdom of God** has no end, neither does it´s revelation or the **Book of Revelation** in itself.

It is up to us to know Him in the revelation of His Glory. It's our duty to discover how to govern with Him and discover our kingship territory. Therefore, this book has no end, it is only the first one God grants me to write, so…….. it shall CONTINUE.

BLESSING

And he said unto me, These sayings are faithful and true: and **the Lord God of the holy prophets** *sent his angel to shew unto his servants the things which must shortly be done.*

Behold, I come quickly: blessed is he that keepeth the sayings of the prophecy of this book. And, behold, I come quickly; and my reward is with me, to give every man according as his work shall be. I am Alpha and Omega, the beginning and the end, the first and the last. Blessed are they that do his commandments, that they may have right to the tree of life, and may enter in through the gates into the city. For without are dogs, and sorcerers, and whoremongers, and murderers, and idolaters, and whosoever loveth and maketh a lie. I Jesus have sent mine angel to testify unto you these things in the churches. I am the root and the offspring of David, and the bright and morning star. And the Spirit and the bride say, Come. And let him that heareth say, Come. And let him that is athirst come. And whosoever will, let him take the water of life freely.

For I testify unto every man that heareth the words of the prophecy of this book, If any man shall add unto these things, God shall add unto him the plagues that are written in this book:

And if any man shall take away from the words of the book of this prophecy, God shall take away his part out of the book of life, and out of the holy city, and from the things which are written in this book.

He which testifieth these things saith, Surely I come quickly. Amen. Even so, come, Lord Jesus.

The grace of our Lord Jesus Christ be with you all. Amen.

Revelation 22:6-7 & 12-21

God is inviting you to be His Wife, so as His Body we overcome and govern jointly with Him. He has prepared a unique and precious revelation about Jesus Christ for you. This is the authority of your reigning and through it, you call the lost world in to drink of Him, the true Waters of Life. We are the Temple of God, the City of the Living God; our doors are continuously open so that anyone who washes their garments can enter in. The Lamb is our Light and we will reign with Him from age to age. If you are truly thirsty, come and drink of the Waters of His Kingdom and you will be satisfied.

Amen.

SECTION 4

APPENDIXES/INSTRUMENTS
(WHICH WILL HELP YOU REACH YOUR OWN CONCLUSIONS)

Instrument # 1

Words Describing Christ's Presence & His Second Coming

Parousia, Epifania, Apocalipsis and Erchomai

These four words are theologically applied when we study Christ's return.

When we referred to the "*power of preconceived ideas*" we found out how these influence our manner of interpreting Scripture. It was revealing to see how even dictionaries in English, Spanish, and other languages distort the meaning of the word *Apocalypses*. Now we find ourselves again with the same dilemma as we try to study these four words.

These are translated respectively as: *Presence* (***Parousia***), *Shinning* (***Epiphany***) and *Revelation* (***Apocalypses***), *Coming (in aoristo tense*[29]*)* (***Erchomai***). Christian dictionaries however, add to each of their meanings a parenthesis, which state: *(applied to the second coming of Christ)*. This thought does not appear in a normal dictionary.

---

[29] *Erchomai. Conjugated in Aoristo which is not future, but a punctual time, undefined and timeless.*

Therefore when we try to find the revelation of said scripture in our religious dictionaries we undeniably run into a phrase which compels us towards a certain direction: the *Second Coming* as a futuristic, unique fact. This eliminates the possibility to interpret that besides the Second Coming of Christ in His resurrected body, there is a "*Coming*" where He is **already** in our midst and that the Old System has been judged.

Let's remember that Jesus spoke to the Jews, and He promised them that He would return, first to make in them His dwelling place and secondly as a way of a Judgment that would put an end to the old priestly order, and also to bring revenge to the blood of the prophets that was shed in Jerusalem.

Let's remember as well that nowhere in the Old Testament, the coming of the Messiah in the flesh is divided in two separate comings, one to save us from sin and another to reign.

These are theologies that came into place and became popular in the late 1800s.

Jesus will come, comes, and is coming in many different ways a forms of apparitions.

So let us analyze these words with a teachable spirit, and let's see what God may be wanting to show to us, and that we have not yet seen with full clarity.

Dr. Ana Méndez Ferrell

1. Parousia (Parousia[30]) - Parousia appears 24 times[31] in the New Testament and in all of them it means *presence*. This is a noun which cannot be conjugated neither is it related to the verb *"to come"*. Most of the time it refers to the Presence of Christ that we can enjoy today.

Jesus has manifested His Presence in many forms. During His *First Coming* He did it in the flesh and in the Old Testament He came in the appearance as *The Angel of The Lord*. Since His ascension to our days, we have manifestations of His Presence in different levels; from a heavy atmosphere charged with His Spirit, which becomes almost tangible, to all the way to totally visible appearances that many of us have been able to see.

Jesus has many forms in His glorified body and His Face transforms in many manners. He had the form of a gardener when He appeared to Mary at the tomb and she did not recognize Him. He took a different form when He walked with His disciples on the road to Emaus and they did not recognize Him either.

He would appear and disappear in their midst and He would walk through walls. John saw Him in one form walking among the candlesticks and in another, dressed in blood riding a white horse. He saw Him as a Lamb and as a Lion.

This is important to know because He is manifesting Himself in many ways to His Church and each one is different.

---

[30] *3952. parousi÷a parousia, par-oo-see'-ah; from the present participle of 3918; a being near, i.e. advent (often, return; specially, of Christ to punish Jerusalem, or finally the wicked); (by implication) physically, aspect: — coming, presence.*

3918. pa¿reimi pareimi, par'-i-mee; from 3844 and 1510 (including its various forms); to be near, i.e. at hand; neuter present participle (singular) time being, or (plural) property: — come, x have, be here, + lack, (be here) present.

[31] *Matthew 24:3, 27, 37 39. 1 Cor. 15:23, 16:15. 2 Cor. 7:6 & 7, 10:10, Phill. 1:26 & 2:12. 1 Tes. 2:19, 3:13, 4:15, 5:23. 2 Tes. 2:1, 2:8, 2:9. James 5:7 & 8. 2 Peter 1:16, 3:4, 3:12. 1 John 2:28*

In the flesh, Jesus was limited to a physical form but in His Glory His forms are infinite.

Let's see how this same word ***parousia*** is used referring to the "*presence*" of Paul and Titus.

Notice that when using this word, it is not referring to a sudden appearance, but to "a presence" among the church.

> *I am glad of the coming (presence-* ***parousia****) of Stephanas and Fortunatus and Achaicus: for that which was lacking on your part they have supplied.*
> *1 Corinthians 16:17*

> *Nevertheless God, that comforteth those that are cast down, comforted us by the coming (****parousia****) of Titus; And not by his coming (****parousia****) only, but by the consolation wherewith he was comforted in you, when he told us your earnest desire, your mourning, your fervent mind toward me; so that I rejoiced the more.*
> *2 Corinthians 7:6-7*

> *For his letters, say they, are weighty and powerful; but his bodily presence (****parousia****) is weak, and his speech contemptible.*
> *2 Corinthians 10:10*

> *That your rejoicing may be more abundant in Jesus Christ for me by my coming (****parousia****) to you again.*
> *Philippians 1:26*

> *Wherefore, my beloved, as ye have always obeyed, not as in my presence (****parousia****) only, but now much more in my absence, work out your own salvation with fear and trembling.*
>
> *Philippians 2:12*

As we study all the scriptures where we find the word ***parousia*** referring to Jesus' coming, we realize most of them can be applied to His presence in our midst, in the form of apparitions, His intense Presence in a meeting, or for the manifestation of His judgments, especially those that came in the year 70 A.D.

Many wonderful things happen when we wait for the manifestation of His Presence in our midst that transform us into His image when we see Him in His glory.

> *Now the Lord is that Spirit: and where the Spirit of the Lord is, there is liberty.*
> *2 Corinthians 3:18*

> *But we all, with open face beholding as in a glass the glory of the Lord, are changed into the same image from glory to glory, even as by the Spirit of the Lord.*
> *2 Corinthians 3:17-18*

The book of the Prophet Malachi also warns us to walk diligently because He comes to us suddenly to cleanse us so an offering in righteousness can be given unto Him. Here the Lord is not talking about a second coming of the Messiah in flesh, but to those precious moments in which God intervenes in the midst of His people to purify us, so he can judge our enemies, as he also did in the year 70 A.D.

> *Behold, I will send my messenger, and he shall prepare the way before me: and the Lord, whom ye seek, shall suddenly come to his temple, even the messenger of the covenant, whom ye delight in: behold, he shall come, saith the LORD of hosts.*

APOCALYPSE The Revelation of Jesus Christ

But who may abide the day of his coming? and who shall stand when he appeareth? for he is like a refiner's fire, and like fullers' soap:

And he shall sit as a refiner and purifier of silver: and he shall purify the sons of Levi, and purge them as gold and silver, that they may offer unto the LORD ***an offering in righteousness.***

Then shall the offering of Judah and Jerusalem be pleasant unto the LORD, as in the days of old, and as in former years.

And I will come near to you to judgment; and I will be a swift witness against the sorcerers, and against the adulterers, and against false swearers, and against those that oppress the hireling in his wages, the widow, and the fatherless, and that turn aside the stranger from his right, and fear not me, saith the LORD of hosts.

Malachi 3:1-5

2. Epiphany[32] **(Epiphaneia)** - This word refers to the *Brightness of His Glory and of His Holiness*. This is the luminosity that manifests on His face when He acts in judgment or in deliverance. It is a synonym of the word **"*Lampo*"** which means "*to illuminate*", and also of the word "***diaphanes***" that means "*a translucent shimmer, one we can see through*".

This is the visible and glorious appearance of Christ, from a glow to a visible appearance; it's His shimmering Holiness that exposes the scum of the hearts, the consuming fire that purifies and brings judgment.

---

[32] *2015. ejpifa¿neia epiphaneia, ep-if-an´-i-ah; manifestation, apparition, glare, from 2016; a manifestation, i.e. (specially) the advent of Christ (past or future): — appearing, brightness.*

This ***epiphaino*** appearing is a manifestation full of light and glory:

> *Even though we once did estimate Christ from a human viewpoint and as a man, yet now [we have such knowledge of Him that] we know Him no longer [in terms of the flesh].*
> *2 Corinthians 5:16 b Amplified*

> *And then shall that wicked one be revealed, whom the Lord shall consume with the spirit of His mouth, and shall destroy with the brightness **(Epiphaneia)** of His coming - **(parousia)** -*
> *2 Thessalonians 2:8 Interlineal-Greek Bible*

In the year 70 A.D. it was the splendor of God's glory that manifested as a lightening to destroy the old city of Jerusalem.

As an application for our days, this shining appears when God judges a city or when He comes to enlighten the understanding of His people.

To those of us who have waged high level wars in the Spirit, this passage is very clear. In my book "***High Level Warfare***" I talk about what I have named "*God's spotlight*". Every war is a Judgment where God makes His Face blaze with a shining glow that brings all things to the light so they are judged. This same fire, which manifests when we fight, then turns towards us to purify us.

> *For they got not the land in possession by their own sword, neither did their own arm save them, but by Thy right hand and Thine arm and **the light of Thy countenance**, because Thou hadst favor unto them.*
> *Psalm 44:3*

A P O C A L Y P S E   The Revelation of Jesus Christ

Turn us again, O LORD God of hosts; **cause Thy face to shine,** *and we shall be saved!*
Psalm 80:19

It's the **Epiphany of Jesus,** the glow of His Face that illuminates us and leads us into all spiritual truth.

For God, who commanded the light to shine out of darkness, hath shined in our hearts to give the light of the knowledge of the glory of God in the face of Jesus Christ.
2 Corinthians 4:6

To those who are intercessors, this manifest glowing, brilliant presence of Jesus is also quite commonplace.

We, who love His Epiphany, are the ones who sanctify ourselves, and whom God trains in His Righteousness to reign with Him. *The Crown of Righteousness* has been reserved for those who understand the judgments of His government.

Henceforth there is laid up for me a crown of righteousness which the Lord, the righteous Judge, shall give me on that Day -- and not to me only, but unto all those also who love His appearing. (diaphanes).

2 Timothy 4:8

As we can see in these Scriptures, they do not refer to a physical manifestation of Christ which would be the word "*prospon*", as we formerly looked at.

3. Apocalypses (Apokalupsis³³) - This word means revelation, illumination, apparition; this is when, either the Father or Jesus reveal something about Himself to the heart of man.

In the ***Book of Revelation***, which is the ***Revelation of Jesus Christ***, we are immersed in His prophetic realm to see and understand His Heavenly character and how He acts; it's when He goes in and takes out from His secret treasures and then brings them out to the light for us. It's also the revelation of the sentences of all His judgments.

> *And Jesus answered and said unto him, "Blessed art thou, Simon Bar-Jonah, for flesh and blood hath not revealed **(apokalupsis)** it unto thee, but My Father who is in Heaven."*
>
> *Matthew 16:17*

It's the revelation of the knowledge of God that will fill the Earth as the waters cover the sea. It's in the revelation of our Messiah that we find all the treasures of God.

> *... that their hearts might be comforted, being knit together in love unto all the riches of the full assurance of understanding, that they may acknowledge the mystery of God, and of the Father, and of Christ, in whom are hid all the treasures of wisdom and knowledge.*
>
> *Colossians 2:2-3*

4. Erchomai - This is the Word we encounter when Scripture talks about Jesus coming in the clouds. To realize what this means, we must understand what "clouds" mean to God. This theme was dealt with when we analyzed the clouds.

---

[33] 602. ajpoka¿luyiß apokalupsis, ap-ok-al'-oop-sis; from 601; disclosure: — appearing, coming, lighten, manifestation, be revealed, revelation.

The key word here is "*coming*" or "*come*", **erchomai** in Greek. This word is found in the original manuscripts in a grammatical tense that does not exist in Spanish or English called "***aoristo***".

Let's look at a definition of this tense as expressed by a language professor, *Justo Fernando Lopez*:

> "The ***aoristo*** expresses a duration that carries no interest for the speaker, it is sometimes of such a brief duration that it is reduced to a point (momentary aspect). The Greek term *aoristo* means '**indefinite, unlimited, without time limit**'. Origin-wise, it was something such as the 'no-time', the verb without a direct temporal translation, something like eternity, or "forever and ever."
>
> The ***aoristo*** denotes an action as occurring in the past without any reference to its progression, without expressing a completed action. The ***aoristo*** simply presents the action without any reference to its duration. The ***aoristo*** doesn't express duration or termination; it is therefore indeterminate, undefined."

The ***aoristo*** is definitely not in a future tense. Jesus was specifically prophesying in this passage that He would come to spiritually and eternally remain in the midst of His people.

INSTRUMENT # 2

THE TIMES THE PRIMITIVE CHURCH LIVED IN

Since ancient times *Jerusalem* was the city that killed the prophets. The crowning of their guilt came when they killed the Son of God. This crime, the greatest one of all humanity, would usher in the great Judgment of the wrath of God over the *City of David*. The *Roman Empire*, joined to the iniquity of the Jewish people of that time period, brought upon the budding Church a great persecution and death.

During the period of 10 Roman Emperors, Christians were thrown to be devoured by the lions; crucified and burnt as heretics. Converting to Jesus implied a sure death and great tribulation. Day to day, the new believers buried their loved ones by the dozen.

The persecution and the conflict among the Jews peaked to an unprecedented war that began in the year 66 A.D. and climaxed with the destruction of *Jerusalem* three and a half years later in the year 70 A.D.

Jesus told his disciples about these approaching difficult times but encouraged them by letting them know He would put an end to that tribulation by bringing forth the manifestation of His Righteousness. The generation that was to crucify Him would assuredly be in lamentation.

From the end of *Matthew Chapter 23* we see Jesus talking about how the guilt of the fathers had to cap its limit; this would happen when Jehovah would avenge the shed blood in *Jerusalem,* from Abel to Zechariah son of Barachiah. These prophets mark the period that was to be judged thereby putting an end to the ancient era.

Jesus made lamentation for the earthly *Jerusalem*, the one of His time period and announced its desolation. *(Matthew 23:32-39)* In the following *Chapter 24* He explains how this destruction would come about.

The main theme in this passage is the destruction of the Temple and of the whole ancient system in order to give way to the new. Jesus does not have to judge the earthly *Jerusalem* again with such devastation, this already happened. If we ignore history and only study the 24th Chapter of Matthew having a preconceived mentality of the "end of the world" happening in the future, in my opinion we will be making a serious mistake.

The Siege and The Destruction of *Jerusalem* in History[34]

We learn about the details of this uprising through the writings of *Flavius Josephus,* a Jewish military chief who after surrendering to the Romans in 67 A.D. went to be a part of General Titus entourage assisting in the development of the expeditions from

---

[34] *Wikipedia*

the Roman ranks. This is therefore *'a testimony of exception'*, of somebody who lived the conflict from the 2 sides.

The first *Jewish-Roman War*, also known as "**The Great Revolt**" was the first of the three main rebellions of the Jews of the *Judean province* against the *Roman Empire* (Jewish-Romans wars) and took place in the years 66 and 73 A.D. It began in the year 66 A.D. initially because of Greek and Jewish religious tensions. It ended when Roman Legions under Titus besieged and destroyed *Jerusalem,* set the Temple on fire in the year 70 A.D., (a three and a half years of conflict), demolished the main Jewish fortresses (especially *Massadah* in the year 73 A.D.) and either enslaved or massacred a great portion of the Jewish population (from 66 A.D. to 73 A.D. makes it a 7 years-conflict).

Fig. 3 - Detail of the Arch of Titus *depicting the stolen treasures from the* Temple of Jerusalem *(The Seven Branch Menorah, the Golden Table of the Shewbread, the Scrolls of the Law, and the Veil from the* Sancta Sanctorum 3*).*

APOCALYPSE The Revelation of Jesus Christ

The Siege on *Jerusalem*

Fig. 4 - The siege and destruction of Jerusalem by the Romans, under the command of Emperor Titus in 70 A.D. Oil on canvas by David Roberts 1850

The siege over **Jerusalem** was tougher than what Titus expected. Upon not being able to break the city's defenses on one single assault, the Roman army was forced to besiege it, establishing a permanent camp just outside the city. Fenced-in, *Jerusalem* lacked sufficient water and food for all those under siege, taking into account that thousands of pilgrims had arrived in the past months to celebrate the Jewish Passover, and now the Romans were forcefully preventing them from leaving the city to the ends that these pilgrims exerted an even greater pressure on their already diminishing supplies.

Inside *Jerusalem*, the people were dying by the thousands of sicknesses and of famine. However the Jewish revolutionaries were not willing to surrender and they would hurl over the wall those pacifists who appeared suspicious.[35]

Some of the Jews wanting to escape the siege and would make covenants with the Romans from the walls to allow them to leave. The Romans would consent to this, but some they let go and others, inspite of their agreements, they would crucify infront of the walls to intimidate them.

One was taken and the other was left. The same thing happened in the fields. This way Jesus prophecies were being fulfilled.

Fig. 5 - Excavated stones belonging to the wall of the 2nd Temple in Jerusalem , demolished by the Roman army. This street is at the base of the Temple walls linking the west and south. Access is determined by the Archaeological Davidson Center in Jerusalem, Israel.

---

[35] *"War of the Jews"* Book V page 362

In the summer of 70 A.D., after demolishing the walls of *Jerusalem*, the Romans entered and looted the city. They attacked the *Antonia fortress* and soon after they occupied the Temple which was set ablaze, they destroyed it on the 9th of the Jewish month of Av of the same year; the *citadel of Herodes* fell the following month."

After King David, the first Jewish King who reigned over it until its destruction by Titus; **one thousand thirty-nine years** went by, and from its founding to its final destruction, two thousand seventy-seven years, and despite everything, neither its antiquity, its riches, or its fame known throughout the Earth, neither the great glory of its religion was of any value to prevent its destruction and its demise. This was then, the end of the siege and the destruction of *Jerusalem*.

They demolished the other city wall in such a manner and leveled it off in such a way that whosoever came by could barely believe it had ever been inhabited.

newlife
christian church

NEW LIFE CHRISTIAN CHURCH
134 MAIN ROAD EMSWORTH HAMPSHIRE PO10 8HA
Tel: +44 (0)1243 371893/373566
Email: office@nlccuk.org   www.newlifechurch.me

be part o

Instrument # 3

The Signs Of The End

The destruction of Jerusalem with its Temple, the wars they were going to face, the horrendous tribulation of the days ahead, were the topics, which Jesus spoke about with His disciples showing them the signs they were to wait for. In **Matthew 24** *(and analogous passages in* **Mark** *and* **Luke***)* we see what was going to happen from the Earth's point of view, and in the ***Book of Revelation*** Jesus shows John how these events would be seen from Heaven. It then becomes important to analyze these facts from these two points of view to understand what Jesus wanted to say.

In order to understand Jesus' prophecies, it is very important to acknowledgethat Jesus' ministry on earth was only to the Jews. Then, what He spoke to them regarding the end of that era, the destruction of the Temple and of the city, He did it to the generation that was alive in His day. He did not know the day or the hour, that the father had determined for that ending and that ocurred 37 years after He prophesied it in the year 70 A.D.

As I said before, if we do not understand that Matthew, Mark, Luke and John are the fulfillment of every prophecy about the Messiah in the Old Testament, and we turn them into the New one, we are completely changing the meaning of what Jesus came to do on the Earth.

He finished His work, and He does not have to rebuild the Temple once again, to destroy it one more time in the future, because someone put the page of the New Testament in the wrong place.

The new Testament should start when Cornelius receives the Holy Spirit. This is the moment the Gospel starts to be spread among the gentiles.

If we separate Jesus from the fulfillment of the Old Testament, we are not reconizing Him as the Messiah of Israel and we are separating Christianity from Judaism.

And, beloved this is a great mistake.

Jesus is the Messiah of Israel and He closes the cycle of History, to start after His ascension, a whole new chapter in humanity.

1. Analysis of Matthew 24 from The Original Interlineal Greek Textual Bible

The main theme in this passage is the *"Destruction of the Temple"* and of the whole Ancient System to make way for the New. **Matthew 24** contains in itself various themes worthy to analyze in depth, which we have already touched upon in previous chapters, so therefore we will now see it in its generic form:

24:1 And Jesus went out and departed from the temple, and His disciples came to Him to show Him the **buildings of the temple***.*

*24:2 And Jesus said unto them, "See ye not all these things? Verily I say unto you, there shall **not be left here one stone upon another that shall not be thrown down.**"*

*24:3 And as He sat upon the Mount of Olives, the disciples came unto Him privately, saying, "Tell us, when shall these things be? And **what shall be the sign of Thy presence (parousia[36]) and of the end of the age**[37] **(aion)**?"*

Matthew 24:1-3 Interlineal Greek Textual Bible

Wanting to know when that *Era* (AION) was going to end, the disciples asked Him that question. The Presence of Jesus here is not about the *Second Coming of Christ* as the Church has conceived it, but the manifestation of His Righteousness.

Jesus had to judge the *Jerusalem* of His days for the death of all the prophets and the sheer wickedness established in all that religious system. He did not appear in the flesh, but His Presence was manifested as a Judgment.

God wants us to open our spirits to understand how He prophesied in different manners on how He would manifest His Coming after His ascension, which we have analyzed in depth with the scriptures.

---

[36] 3952. parousi÷a pabrousia, par-oo-see'-ah; from the present participle of 3918; a being near, i.e. advent (often, return; specially, of Christ to punish Jerusalem, or finally the wicked); (by implication) physically, aspect: — coming, presence.

[37] 165. aijw¿n aion, ahee-ohn'; propiamente, una era from the same as 104; properly, an age; by extension, perpetuity (also past); by implication, the world; specially (Jewish) a Messianic period (present or future): — age, course, eternal, (for) ever(-more), (n-)ever, (beginning of the , while the) world (began, without end). Compare 5550.

He then speaks to them on how that moment would come about when God would act in His wrath devastating the city. Upon God judging the former age, The Kingdom of God would manifest and remain established.

And Jesus answered and said unto them, "Take heed that no man deceive you; for many shall come in My name, saying, `I am Christ,' and shall deceive many. And ye shall hear of wars and rumors of wars. See that ye be not troubled, for all these things must come to pass, but the end is not yet.

For nation shall rise against nation and kingdom against kingdom, and there shall be famines and pestilences and earthquakes in divers places.

All these are the beginning of sorrows. Then **shall they deliver you up to be afflicted and shall kill you**, *and ye shall be hated by all nations for My name's sake.*
Matthew 24:4-13   --- ???

Since the time of the **Acts of the Apostles**, Christians were persecuted and killed as I previously mentioned. Added to this were the internal wars between Jews who came from diverse parts of the land. John himself mentions this tribulation in the year 64[38] when he writes the **Book of Revelation**.

---

[38] *Some think the Book of Revelation was written in the year 95 D.C., but this theory fails on its own because the Temple was destroyed in the year 70 and Chaper 11 predicts its destruction. More accurate theories place it between 64 and 67 D.C. which is much more logical due to the content of the book.*

Dr. Ana Méndez Ferrell

> *I, John, who also am your brother and companion in the **tribulation and in the Kingdom and in the patience of Jesus Christ**, was on the isle that is called Patmos, for the Word of God and for the testimony of Jesus Christ.*
>
> *Revelation 1:9*

After the resurrection, Jesus took up the throne and sat as Lord of lords, however the Father establishes a time mentioned in the Bible as the *"time of His patience"* or *"the time of the patience of Jesus Christ"* in which He gives all the Jewish people an opportunity of salvation before releasing His judgment over the Old Jerusalem.

> *24:13 And then shall many lose faith and shall betray one another and shall hate one another. And many false prophets shall rise and shall deceive many. And because iniquity shall abound, the love of many shall wax cold. But he that shall endure unto the end,* [39] *(**Greek: telos, appointed time**) same shall be saved.*
>
> *24:14 And this Gospel of the Kingdom shall be preached in all the inhabited land (all the world) for a witness unto all nations, and then shall **the end of the age** come.*
>
> *Matthew 24:13-14 emphasis added by the author*

---

[39] 5056. te÷loß telos,) tel´-os; from a primary te÷llw tello (to set out for a definite point or goal); properly, the point aimed at as a limit, i.e. (by implication) the conclusion of an act or state (termination (literally, figuratively or indefinitely), result (immediate, ultimate or prophetic), purpose; specially, an impost or levy (as paid): — + continual, custom, end(-ing), finally, uttermost. Compare 5411.

APOCALYPSE The Revelation of Jesus Christ

We have two interesting groups of words to analyze here:

"All the inhabited land" (all the world) In the original Greek we find the words **"*eis*"** and **"*oikoumene*"**,[40] which mean: *a territory or a portion of the globe*. It was also used to determine the *Roman Empire* territory. This is why Paul addresses the Romans in this fashion:

> *But I ask, have they not heard? Yes, verily: "Their sound went out into all the earth, and their words **unto the ends of the world**."*
> *Romans 10:18*

> *...which has come unto you, as it has **in all the world**, and bringeth forth fruit, as it doth also in you since the day ye heard of it and knew the grace of God in truth.*
> *Colossians 1:6*

Jesus here is not talking in the context of the *preaching of the Gospel to all the Earth*, He was referring to the territory to where Judgment was coming which was the *Roman Empire* and the Old Covenant.

> *When ye therefore shall see the abomination of desolation, spoken of by Daniel the prophet, standing in the holy place (whosoever readeth, let him understand),*
> *Matthew 24:15*

Jesus calls us to understand something about this verse in **Matthew** that *"the abomination of desolation"* was not just an

---

[40] 1519. eijß, eis ice; a primary preposition; to or into 3625 oijkoume÷nh oikoumene oy-kou-men´-ay; feminine participle present passive of 3611 (as noun, by implication, of 1093); land, i.e. the (terrene part of the) globe; specially, the Roman Empire: — earth, world.

isolated event that was soon going to happen, but it was something that had happened, and would repeatedly happen.

When Daniel interpreted Nebuchadnezzar's dream, he saw a great statute formed by four empires: the *Babylon*ian, the Mede-Persian, the Greek and the Roman. In another of his visions he again sees these same kingdoms represented by the four beasts, which came and conquered Israel.

The *abomination of the desolation* occurs in three of these Empires:

1. The temple is defiled by the Babylonian gods. Ezekiel sees the statue of Tammuz in the Holy Place and abominations written in the walls of the Temple. *(Ezekiel 8)*

2. In the year 164 BC Antiochus IV Epiphanes, Greek Emperor whose name means, "god manifested," ordered the profanation of the *Temple of Jerusalem*. He ordered a statue of Zeus be placed in the Holy of Holies and abominable things such as a pig be sacrificed upon the Altar.

3. The Temple was defiled during the wars of the Jews between 66 and 70 A.D. John of Giscala, a thief and a murderer that was one of the leaders of the Jewish civil war, made the Temple his headquarters. Also before the temple was destroyed in the year 70 AD, pagan soldiers penetrated the Temple and put at the door the Emperor's symbols. Some theologians allude that the *abomination of the desolation* was fulfilled at that moment since according to Jewish Law nothing impure could penetrate the Temple.

We see through these events how *"the abomination of desolation"* took place on several occasions when ungodly people profaned the Temple.

In my opinion, Jesus was not only talking about one single act but about a repetitive pattern, which ended with the destruction of *Jerusalem*.

In Daniel's interpretation about this statue Nebuchadnezzar dreamt, Jesus is The Rock he sees coming out of the sky and destroying it by striking its iron and clay feet, which represent the *Roman Empire*.

> *Thou sawest until a stone was cut out without hands, which smote the image upon his feet that were of iron and clay, and broke them to pieces. Then were the iron, the clay, the brass, the silver, and the gold broken to pieces together, and became like the chaff of the summer threshing floors; and the wind carried them away, that no place was found for them.* **And the stone that smote the image became a great mountain and filled the whole earth.**
>
> Daniel 2:34-35

John, in his **Book of Revelation** visions, sees the heavenly fulfillment of that moment when he describes the fall of the great *Babylon*, which is the compendium of those four empires. Jesus is the Rock that came out from Heaven bringing the authority of His Kingdom to destroy the system of the world.

> *Then a mighty angel took up a stone like a great millstone and threw it into the sea, saying, "Thus with violence the great city Babylon shall be thrown down, and shall not be found anymore.*
>
> Revelation 18:21

Mount Zion is the government of God that fills the whole Earth with His Righteousness. This is The Mountain above all mountains and the Kingdom above all kingdoms.

The **Mountain of the Lord** is already all over the planet. This happened with the destruction of the *Roman Empire*. This is why it is written that we have approached *Mount Zion*, not the physical mount in Israel but the one that fills the Earth.

> *But ye are come unto mount Zion, and unto the city of the living God, the heavenly Jerusalem, and to an innumerable company of angels.*
> *Hebrews 12:22*

Now let's go back to our study of **Matthew 24** where Jesus is going to warn His disciples about the time of their escape from *Jerusalem*.

THE ESCAPE

It is historically known that during the first century the Church fled to the mountains to save their lives by heeding Jesus' warning when *Jerusalem* was conquered.

Now going back to **Matthew 24**:

> *...then let them that be in Judea flee unto the mountains. Let him that is on the housetop not come down to take anything out of his house; neither let him that is in the field return back to take his clothes. And woe unto them that are with child, and to them that give suck in those days!*
> *But pray ye that your flight be not in the winter, neither* **on the Sabbath day**.
> *Matthew 24; 16-20*

The fact that He alluded to the '*day of rest*' clearly shows us He was referring to the Jews of His time period and not to the Church composed of Jews and Gentiles. For the Church, Jesus is our '*day of rest.*'

> *For if Joshua had given them **rest**, then He would not afterward have spoken of another day.*
> *There remains therefore a **rest** for the people of God. For he who has entered His **rest** has himself also ceased from his works as God did from His.*
> *Hebrews 4:8-10*

> *Let no man therefore judge you in meat or drink, or in respect to a holy day or the new moon or the Sabbath days, which are a shadow of things to come, but the body is of Christ.*
> *Colossians 2:16-17*

We cannot place this '*escape*' twenty-one centuries in the future, as the non-Jewish Church does not celebrate the Sabbath, neither is this part of the New Testament doctrine preached by the Apostles to the gentiles.

When Jesus was carrying the Cross He spoke to the women who were weeping for Him about the difficult times that were at hand.

> *But Jesus, turning unto them, said, Daughters of Jerusalem, weep not for Me, but weep for yourselves and for your children. For behold, the days are coming in which they shall say, `Blessed are the barren, and the wombs that never bore and the breasts which never gave suck.'"*
> *Luke 23:28-29*

He was not referring to women thousands of years later but to those who were weeping at that moment because He knew of the impending destruction and how difficult it would be for them to flee under those conditions.

We cannot place the escape twenty-one centuries later when the non-Jewish Church does not keep "the day of rest" nor does it form part of the Neo-Testamentary doctrine to the gentiles.

> *For then shall be great tribulation, such as was not since the beginning of the world to this time, no, nor ever shall be.*
> *Matthew 24:21*

Jesus was referring to a time of tribulation that would take place in the 37 years between His resurrection and the fall of *Jerusalem*.

These were the wars among the Jews and the persecution of Christians. Further on I will talk about the great tribulation from the heavenly point of view in the **Book of Revelation**.

> *And unless those days should be shortened, there should no flesh be saved; but for the elect's sake, those days shall be shortened.*
>
> *Then if any man shall say unto you, `Lo, here is Christ,' or `there,' believe it not.*
>
> *For there shall arise false chrisms and false prophets and shall show great signs and wonders, insomuch that, if it were possible, they shall deceive the very elect.*

> *Behold, I have told you before. Therefore, if they shall say unto you, `Behold, He is in the desert!' go not forth; or `Behold, He is in the secret chambers!' believe it not.*
>
> *For as the lightning cometh out of the east and shineth even unto the west, so shall also the **presence** (Parousia) of the Son of Man be.*
>
> *Matthew 24:22-27*

This word *"parousia"* in verse 27 is the same as in 24:3 where Jesus is talking about the manifestation of His Righteousness, not about a physical appearance.

The comparison Jesus intends to make is not to the rushing speed of a thunderbolt but to its light that illuminates the whole sky in the midst of the darkness produced by a storm. He is talking about the influence of His presence (***parousia***) bringing illumination to the conscience as the brightness of lightning lights up the whole sky.

Jesus is explaining that the manifested Righteousness of His Presence (***parousia***) was not something private or hidden but something that was to be obviously recognized by *Israel*. He was not going to be as the false Christs who hide in the desert and in their secret chambers but His light would greatly influence and shine over all humanity and His judgments visible to every eye.

In a parallel verse in *Luke 17* the Textual Bible says:

Dr. Ana Méndez Ferrell

For as the lightning that lighteneth from one extreme to the other in heaven and **where the Heavens join with the Earth, so shall also the Son of Man be in His day.**

Luke 17:24 Textual Bible

This verse affirms what Paul says about the union of Heaven and Earth in Jesus *(Ephesians 1:9)*. This is the living essence of the Kingdom that opens up for us the heavenly dimensions within Him.

For wheresoever the carcass is, there will the eagles be gathered together.

Matthew 24:28

This refers to the great slaughter that was to come. As *Flavio Josephus* wrote in **"The Wars of the Jews"** the corpses were piled up by the thousands in the streets of Jerusalem. Eagles in this case are a symbol of the Roman armies. The Jews who were left in *Israel* who did not convert to Christ took refuge at the fortress of *Massadah* where they committed mass suicide, in order not to be killed by the Romans who had put a siege around them.

24:29 Immediately after the tribulation of those days shall the sun be darkened and the moon shall not give her light, and the stars shall fall from heaven and the powers of the heavens shall be shaken.

Matthew 24:29 Interlineal Greek Textual Bible

This passage is parallel to the one in *2 Peter 3:9 and 10* we previously studied, where the powers of darkness and the structures of this world were judged to make a way for the new Era of the government of Christ.

JESUS COMES IN THE CLOUDS

*24:30 and then shall appear the sign of the Son of Man in heaven. And then shall all the tribes of the earth[41] **(ghv ge,** ghay), mourn, and they shall see the Son of Man coming[42] **(ercomai erchomai)** in the clouds of heaven with power and with great glory.*

Matthew 24:30 Interlineal Greek Textual Bible

Let's be reminded that at the beginning of this Chapter Jesus unites *"The sign of His Coming"* with the *"End of the Age."*

We will first analyze the word *"coming"* since we already analyzed the word *"cloud"* in Chapter 13.

The word *"coming"* is key here, *"**erchomai**"* in Greek. This is found in the original manuscripts in a grammar tense that doesn't exist in English or Spanish named ***"aoristo."*** We analyzed this word in *Appendix/Instrument # 1*.

Here again, ***aoristo*** is definitely not a word of the future tense. Jesus was specifically prophesying in this passage that He was to come to stay spiritually and eternally amidst His people. In other words, it is talking here about a manifestation of Christ where He makes His Glory and Great Power radiate limitlessly from Eternity with the purpose to judge the iniquity that would bring an end to that age.

---

[41] *1093. ghv ge, ghay; contracted from a primary word; soil; by extension a region, or the solid part or the whole of the terrene globe (including the occupants in each application): — country, earth(-ly), ground, land, world.*

[42] *2064. e¶rcomai erchomai, er'-khom-ahee; middle voice of a primary verb (used only in the present and imperfect tenses, the others being supplied by a kindred (middle voice)*

As of that moment, Jesus is endlessly and throughout the ages and ages manifesting Himself in the life of His Church and putting His enemies as His footstool.

> *For where two or three are gathered together in My name, there am I in the midst of them."*
> *Matthew 18:20*

Remember that nowhere in the Old Testament were two different comings of the Messiah prophecied.

Jesus never did or said anything that was not written and foretold in the Sciptures. He specifically declared that His Kingdom was not of this world.

The passage of Matthew 24:30 about Jesus coming in the clouds is parallel to *Revelation 1:7:*

> *Behold, He cometh (**erchomai**) with clouds, and every eye shall see Him, and they also who pierced Him; and all kindreds of the earth shall wail because of Him. Even so. Amen.*
> *Revelation 1:7*

The angel of the Lord was announcing to His people through John that Jesus was about to manifest His Glory coming to judge those who had pierced Him and those who were murdering the brethren. These were news of great joy for the Church living in great tribulation.

Jesus was quoting the passage prophesied by *Zechariah*:

> *And I will pour upon the house of David and upon the inhabitants of Jerusalem the spirit of grace and of supplication;* ***and they shall look upon Me whom they have pierced****, and they shall mourn for Him as one mourneth for his only son, and shall be in bitterness for Him as one who is in bitterness for his firstborn.*
>
> Zechariah 12:10

This whole passage of *Zechariah* talks about the ensuing lamentation to occur when *Jerusalem* was to be destroyed in the year 70. Jesus was not talking about innocent Jews twenty-one centuries afterwards; He was referring to those who literally pierced Him.

In a spiritual sense this also applies to us when we experience His ***"erchomai"***, that punctual moment in which Eternity manifested in our lives. When Christ comes to us and reveals to our hearts His suffering at the Cross, the Holy Spirit convicts us of sin and we necessarily grieve for Him upon realizing that we ourselves pierced Him by our iniquities.

THE CLOUDS

I dedicated this book's chapter 13 to this topic, which is of radical importance. As of now, let's remain in the idea of the analysis of *Matthew 24* that Jesus is talking about a manifestation of His Presence that would bring an end to the Temple in *Jerusalem* and to the Ancient Era. In the same manner Jehovah manifested as a pillar of cloud and fire, now He would manifest to judge the *Babylon*ic system that had corrupted the entire priestly order of the Old Testament.

And He shall send His angels with a great sound of a trumpet, and they shall gather together His elect from the four winds, from one end of heaven to the other.

"Now learn a parable of the fig tree: When his branch is yet tender and putteth forth leaves, ye know that summer is nigh.

So likewise ye, when ye shall see all these things, know that it is near, even at the doors.

Verily I say unto you, this generation shall not pass till all these things be fulfilled.

Heaven and earth shall pass away, but My Words shall not pass away.

Matthew 24:31-35

Jesus was speaking to THAT generation who would experience a horrendous persecution, not to a generation two thousand years later. That generation was to suffer the intense persecution and killing of the first Christians, the many conflicts among the Jews, the intense war that started on the year 66 and the siege over *Jerusalem*.

Biblically speaking, a generation encompasses 40 years. He was talking to them. He was preparing them for what they were about to undergo. He placed a sense of urgency on them, which we repeatedly read in the first three chapters of **Book of Revelation**: "*things which must shortly come to pass*", "*I come quickly*", "*Behold I stand at the door and knock*". Time was running out and they had to hurry up and preach left and right because many would be lost.

> *But of that day and hour, knoweth no man, no, not the angels of Heaven, but My Father only.*
>
> *But as the days of Noah were, so shall also the coming of the Son of Man be.*
>
> *For as in the days that were before the flood they were eating and drinking, marrying and giving in marriage, until the day that Noah entered into the ark and knew not until the flood came and took them all away, so shall also the coming (parousia) of the Son of Man be.*
>
> *Matthew 24:36-39*

These verses speak to us about the lack of reverence and unbelief from the people towards the words of their Messiah. Just as Noah went unheeded and everyone did as they pleased, likewise many of the Jewish people responded to the words of Jesus.

> *Then shall two be in the field; the one shall be taken and the other left.*
> *Two women shall be grinding at the mill; the one shall be taken and the other left.*
> *Matthew 24:40-41*

Many of the Jews who were trapped inside Jerusalem during the siege, would make agreements with the Romans to let them escape. The Romans allowed them to run away, but some they let go free and others were taken to be crucified. The same thing happened with those who were found outside Jerusalem, in the fields or their farms.

One was taken and the other left.

Jesus was quoting *Zechariah's* prophecy and how one out of two were going to be taken captives.

> *For I will gather all nations against Jerusalem to battle; and the city shall be taken, and the houses rifled, and the women ravished. And half of the city shall go forth into captivity, and the residue of the people shall not be cut off from the city* **where half of the citizens shall be taken captive and the rest will not.**
>
> *Zechariah 14:2*

Every prophecy about Jesus is coherent and must be confirmed according to the Old Testament because it was He, Himself who prophesied about Himself through the prophets.

> *Of this salvation the prophets have inquired and searched carefully, who prophesied of the grace that would come to you, searching what, or what manner of time,* **the Spirit of Christ who was in them** *was indicating when He testified beforehand the sufferings of Christ and the glories that would follow.*
>
> *1 Peter 1:10-11*

There is no passage in the Old Testament where the Messiah is seen disappearing anybody from the planet as many have interpreted this scriptural passage. I consider it is necessary and encourage you to take into account He who prophesied all things, Who is Christ, to reach a truthful conclusion of what He spoke to us:

> "Watch therefore, for ye know not what hour your Lord doth come. (erchomai)
>
> *Matthew 24:42*

The verb is conjugated in ***aoristo,*** indicating to us again the surprising and eternal Presence of when the Lord would then come.

> "But know this, that if the master of the house had known in what watch the thief would come, he would have watched and would not have suffered his house to be broken into.
>
> Therefore be ye also ready, for in such an hour as ye think not, the Son of Man cometh.
>
> "Who then is a faithful and wise servant, whom his lord hath made ruler over his household, to give them meat in due season?
>
> Blessed is that servant whom his lord, when he cometh, shall find so doing.
>
> Verily I say unto you, that he shall make him ruler over all his goods.
>
> But if that evil servant shall say in his heart, `My lord delayeth his coming,'
>
> and shall begin to smite his fellow servants and to eat and drink with the drunken,

the lord of that servant shall come in a day when he looketh not for him, and in an hour that he is not aware of,
and shall cut him asunder and appoint him his portion with the hypocrites: there shall be weeping and gnashing of teeth. (And this Gospel of the Kingdom shall be preached in all the world as a testimony to the nations, and then shall the end come.)
Matthew 24:43-51

Jesus finishes His speech by urging them to persevere in their faithfullness. The second part of this last verse does not appear in the originals.

These verses were an encouragement to the early believers; they are also alive for us as a fundamental principle of our spiritual life. Jesus will always come to us manifesting His Presence in our heartsthrough His glorious apparitions and He dwells in our midst.

I will not leave you orphans; I will come to you. "A little while longer and the world will see Me no more, but you will see Me. Because I live, you will live also.
At that day you will know that I am in My Father, and you in Me, and I in you.
John 14:18-20

Teaching them to observe everything that I have commanded you, and behold, I am with you all the days (perpetually, uniformly, and on every occasion), to the [very] close and consummation of the age. Amen (so let it be).
Matthew 28:20 Amplified

APOCALYPSE The Revelation of Jesus Christ

When Jesus spoke these words He was physically in the world, therefore He could not live in the hearts of His disciples. He was telling them that He would come to dwell in our midst, and that His Presence (**parousia**) would live in our hearts.

He said to Paul when He appeared to him in the way to *Damascus* that He will appear to him many times in the same manner.

> *But rise and stand on your feet; for I have appeared to you for this purpose, to make you a minister and a witness both of the things which you have seen and of the things which I will yet reveal to you.*
>
> *Acts 26:16*

Instrument # 4

The Intermediate coming of Christ

by Apostle Fernando Orihuela

The teaching about a secret coming before the manifestation of the man of sin has been much taught -and believed- in the 20th century. The majority of Christians have accepted this with little or no research. Regardless of how impacting it may sound, this teaching was not the position of the primitive Church, or the Reformers, or anybody's, until around the year 1830. If this were true, the teaching about a secret rapture before the tribulation is not part of the original faith given to the saints.

After looking at the big picture of the Church's history, Professor George Ladd stated: "All the Church fathers who write about this matter think the Church will suffer at the hands of the antichrist…we cannot find any trace of pre-tribulationism in the primitive church and not one of the modern pre-tribulationists have proven that this doctrine was believed in by any of the church fathers or by any of the students of the Word before the XIX century."[43]

Many accredited men of God who stand out in Christian history: *John Wyclif, John Huss, Martin Lutero, Phillip Melanchton, Huldreich Zwinglio, William Tyndale, Nicholas Ridley, Hugh Latimer, John Fox, Edwin Sandys, Jacobo Calvino, John Knox, Isaac Newton, John Wesley*; none of these men believed the Church would be removed before the manifestation of the antichrist. They believed that the Church would suffer at the hands of the antichrist, whose career would then end with Christ's coming.

What is nowadays taught with great confidence is that the rapture will take away the saved to Heaven before the antichrist and before the coming of Christ in power and glory. What few people know is that this doctrine's origin is comparatively modern.

Edward Irving was born in *Scotland* in 1792. An eloquent preacher with a remarkable anointing, by 1828 his open-air meetings attracted more than 10,0000 people. Hundreds filled his church week after week. In 1832 he wrote a treatise that suggested Jesus had a fallen human nature. This caused such a great controversy amidst his congregation that he was removed from his pulpit. An ecclesiastical trial in 1833 took away his status as clergyman from the *Church of Scotland* and he passed away the following year in *Glasgow*.[44]

On September 1830, Irving's journal, "*The Morning Watch*" published an article that introduced a two-phased idea regarding the coming of Christ. Many believe the seeds of this doctrine came from a Spanish book: "*The Coming of Messiah in Glory and*

---

[43] George E. Ladd, The Blessed Hope (Grand Rapids: Eerdmans, 1956), page 31

[44] LeRoy E. Froom, The Prophetic faith of Our Fathers (Washington: Review and Herald 1945), Vol. 3, p.516.

Majesty" written by Manuel Lacunza – a priest and Jesuit Chilean theologian born in 1731 who performed a millennialism interpretation of the Catholic Bible prophecies[45] - which was translated into English by Irving in 1827.[46] This book originally published in 1812 stated: "when the Lord shall come from Heaven to Earth, upon His coming, and long before His arrival to Earth, shall give His command and sent His mandates...with a shout...with the voice of the archangel and with the trump of God. Those who hear this voice of the Son of God shall resurrect right away." [47]

Shortly thereafter, the secret coming was taught among a group named the *Plymouth Brethren* and to be precise, it was accepted by some and rejected by others. In 1864, S.P. Tregelles, one of the brethren who rejected this teaching wrote: "I was not aware of the existence of any definite teaching about a Church's secret rapture by a secret coming until this was introduced "in a prophecy" in Mr. Irving's church which was perceived as the voice of the Spirit. But whether anybody was right about it or not, it arose from that alleged revelation along with a modern doctrine and modern phraseology. It came, not from the Holy Spirit, but from one who feigned to be the Spirit of God".[48]

Curiously enough, this new revelation - the teaching about a separate coming to take away those who were ready - was to be dogmatically defended as if it had always been an eternal truth from Scripture. In the years to follow, this two-phased coming teaching was developed by John Nelson Darby (1800-1882).

---

[45] http://es.wikipedia.org/wiki/Manuel_Lacunza, researched on September 2011

[46] John L. Bray, *The Origin of the Pre-Tribulation Rapture Teaching* (Lakeland, FL: John L. Bray Ministry, Inc., 1982).

[47] Manuel de lacunza, *The Coming of Messiah in Glory and Majesty* (London: translated by Irving, 1827), Vol 1, p.99.

[48] S.P.Tregelles, *The Hope of Christ's Second Coming* (London: Samuel Bagster and Sons, 1864), pp.34-37.

He became a leader among the *Plymouth Brethren*, a movement composed of people who became disappointed with the sleepy condition that prevailed in many of the churches.

At the end, through the *Scofield Bible*, many ended up believing in a secret rapture. Oswald J. Smith was one of them but later wrote: "Now after many years of studying and praying, I am absolutely convinced that there will be no taking away before the tribulation. I simply believed in another theory because I was taught by W.E. Blackstone's book *"Jesus is Coming,"* Scofield's Bible, the prophetic conferences and the bible schools, but when I began scrutinizing Scripture, I discovered that there was no verse that supported the pre-tribulation theory."[49]

Presently, this teaching is repeated by hundreds of ministers throughout the world without knowing exactly its origin.

W. E. Blackstone says that one can read in the *Book of the Acts of the Apostles*:

> *Repent ye therefore and be converted, that your sins may be blotted out when the times of refreshing shall come from the presence of the Lord. Then He shall send Jesus Christ, who before was preached unto you, whom Heaven must receive until the times of restitution of all things, which God hath spoken by the mouth of all His holy prophets since the world began*
>
> Acts 3:19-21

The word "restitution" is Greek is **apokatástasis,** this word comes from **apo** which means "*in return*, or *once again*" and **katastemi,** which means "put in order."[50]

---

[49] *Smith, op.cit., pp.2,3.*

[50] *Strong's Concordance G605.*

Dr. Ana Méndez Ferrell

We are undeniably living these times of restoration since God is raising scholars and ministers who have the boldness to revisit subject matters that are the objects of discussion. Certainly the Eschatology matter is one that carries the most doubts and yet the least one men like to tackle simply because the price is too steep. Many doors shall close simply because the revelation-less church has lost its capacity to reflect about the things it believes. Unfortunately, doctrinal tradition weighs so heavily that it is even above the principles of love and respect; many people so to speak, shall rupture their friendship with another minister solely because one has changed their thinking about a doctrinal issue.

INSTRUMENT # 5

THE ORDER OF THE BOOK OF REVELATION

I want to propose what appears to be the logical order to understand the **Book of Revelation**.

As I previously stated, this is not a chronological book. The judgments and heavenly scenes are occurring simultaneously in God's timeless realm.

I also want to remind you that when the Canon was put together, the different parts of the **Book of Revelation** were not in order. Men were the ones who established its chapters and titles.

Some of these have been placed according to the interpretation they wanted to give it and upon reading it they compel the reader to a determinate interpretation. These titles do not form part of the Word revealed by God.

This order is only a suggestion; it is by no means an imposition or an immovable truth:

APOCALYPSE The Revelation of Jesus Christ

Chapter 1	*The Revelation of Jesus Christ*
Chapters 2 - 3	*The Message to the Seven Churches*
Chapter 4	*The Heavenly Vision*
Chapter 5	*The Lion and the Lamb*
Chapter 6	*The Seven Seals*
Chapter 7	*The Sealed and the Great Multitude*
Chapter 8	*The Seven Trumpets*
Chapter 9	*The Trumpets Continue*
Chapter 10	*The Two Olives and the Wrath of God* *(11th in the Bible)*
Chapter 11	*The Woman and the Dragon* (12th in the Bible)
Chapter 12	*The Dragon and the Beasts* (13th in the Bible)
Chapter 13	*The Judgment of Babylon* (17th in the Bible)
Chapter 14	*The Judgment of Babylon Continues* (18th in the Bible)

Chapter 15	*The New Song of the 144,000, the Three Angels and the Wine Press* (14th in the Bible)
Chapter 16	*The Seven Plagues* (15th in the Bible)
Chapter 17	*The Seven Vials of Wrath* (16th in the Bible)
Chapter 18	*The Kingdom and the Wife Established in Heaven* (19th in the Bible)
Chapter 19	*The New Jerusalem, Christ's Wife* (21st in the Bible)
Chapter 20	*Continues the Description of the New Jerusalem until Verse 5* (22nd in the Bible)
Chapter 21	*The Kingdom is Spiritual and satan Cannot Touch It* (20th in the Bible up to verse 10)
Chapter 22	*The Final Judgment Chapter 22* (20th in the Bible, beginning with verse 11th)
Chapter 23	*The Angel and the Little Book and the Epilogue* (10th and 22:6-21 in the Bible)

Participate in our On Demand Courses

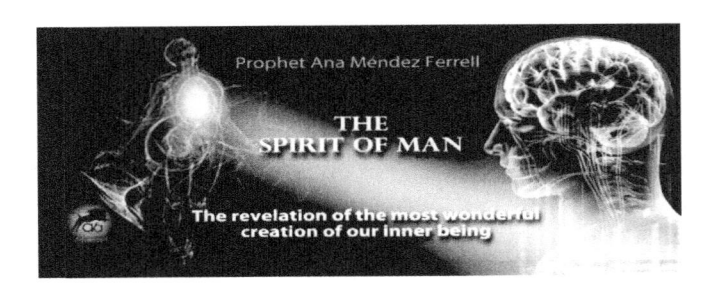

THE SPIRIT OF MAN
Prophet Ana Méndez Ferrell
The revelation of the most wonderful creation of our inner being

GOVERNING IN THE SPIRIT
A Time for Kings to rule with righteousness
NOW ON-DEMAND

The Consciousness of Christ Series

at.votlm.com

If you enjoyed reading this book, we also recommend

Regions of Captivity

Shaking the Heavens

Pharmakeia

The Dark Secret of G.A.O.T.U.

www.voiceofthelight.com

You can watch us online

on our channel

Frequencies of Glory TV

Powerful messages and worship

www.frequenciesofglorytv.com

Follow us on Facebook

Voice Of The Light Ministries

www.voiceofthelight.com

904-834-2447

P.O. Box 3418

Ponte Vedra, FL. 32004

USA

Printed in Great Britain
by Amazon